EVANGELISM
A
Reformed
Debate

EVANGELISM
A
Reformed
Debate

JOHN KENNEDY

HORATIUS BONAR

The James Begg Society

THE JAMES BEGG SOCIETY

ISBN 0-9526799-1-4

For information about the Society please contact:-

Mr. Paul Hayden (Secretary)
67 Ffordd Garnedd
Portdinorwic
N. Wales
LL56 4QY.

Printed in Great Britain by
Redwood Books, Trowbridge, Wiltshire

Contents

———

PART 3
KENNEDY: A REPLY

Preface

EVANGELISM is a must for the Church. She has a divine imperative and a heavenly mandate for this labour of love. Scripture says *"Go ye into all the world, and preach..."*; this means that an extensive part of her theology is the theology of mission. In this the Scottish Kirk has been unsurpassed historically. Every minister is a missionary to the souls under his care, and he yearns and prays for revival in the lives of his people. The Church then must be a Church in mission. Unless she evangelises she will fail her Lord. And unless she sows **obediently** there will be no harvest.

This century the Church has gone through trial and error in evangelism. There is nothing knew in this. Dr. Kennedy last century observed a novel departing from the old conception of the Church, to a new idea of making her "relevant" and "successful." Success which was in his view however, at the expense of faithfulness. He differed with most of his countrymen in the *modus operandi* of evangelism.

The renowned revivalists have indeed failed. Thousands upon thousands have professed Christ, but Britain has grown more and more godless. If the tree is to be known by her fruit, then the new evangelicalism is exposed as counterfeit: its products do not have the weight, attractiveness and savour of the old.

There were big fish as well as minnows debating with Kennedy, but we can see today the fruit they left behind; a weakened Christianity unable to withstand the world which it must encounter. The Church must face the fact that the Reformed Faith remains robust while other forms crumble. Biblical religion alone will endure the storm; all else is built upon sand.

A true turning to God in the land is always marked by a hunger for the word purely-preached and unadorned by the fashions and sentimentalities of the age; by a calling upon God as the supreme Sovereign and our chiefest good; and by the giving of glory to Him in the offering of praise. Every endeavour to advance the "glorious gospel of the blessed God" must promote these elements for a successful outcome pleasing to the Lord. It is the church's great privilege that she is Christ's appointed agent for the gathering of His scattered sheep: that this volume might be of guidance to her in her sacred task is the earnest longing and prayer of the publishers.

The three pamphlets which comprised the debate are here reproduced under one title for the first time. The cover-pages of the originals are reproduced at the beginning of each part, and an Index to the main subjects has been added.

We extend our grateful thanks to many who have helped in the production of the present work, particularly to Rev. Professor Hugh M. Cartwright of the Free Church College, Edinburgh, for writing the Introduction. Our greatest indebtedness as ever is to Almighty God for His abounding mercy and grace.

L ORD, bless and pity us,
 shine on us with thy face:
That th' earth thy way, and
  nations all
 may know thy saving grace.
Let people praise thee, Lord;
 let people all thee praise.
O let the nations be glad,
 in songs their voices raise:

Thou'lt justly people judge,
 on earth rule nations all.
Let people praise thee, Lord; let them
 praise thee, both great and small.
The earth her fruit shall yield,
 our God shall blessing send.
God shall us bless; men shall him fear
 unto earth's utmost end.

Psalm 67.

Introduction

TO some these three pamphlets may seem relics of theological battles fought long ago on a field as distant from us in relevance as in time. But those who read carefully will see, behind the local and temporary, the spiritual war of which these battles formed a part and which goes on still. There can be advantage in considering contemporary issues as they were discussed in previous manifestations. The perspective given by subsequent history helps to illustrate the accuracy of assessments made on Biblical grounds of the real tendency of movements which, though applauded at the time, involved serious departures from Biblical truth and practice.

Moody and Sankey appeared in Scotland when the churches, surrounded by unchurched masses, were complaining of spiritual stagnation and were seeking to accommodate themselves intellectually, doctrinally and liturgically to the spirit of the age in order to win the age. The Calvinism of the Westminster Confession was giving place to something closer to Arminianism. For different reasons Biblical critics and devout men like Dr. Bonar could join in supporting a movement which, whatever effect it had on the unchurched masses, seemed to 'bring to decision' multitudes of previously nominal or fringe adherents of the churches.

Kennedy contends for the Word of God as the only standard for regulating the theological content of preaching and the method of evangelism. He argues that aims and results do not justify unbiblical doctrines and means and that however excited even good men may become over the seeming success of such they will pervert and replace Biblical Christianity. "A negative theology will soon supplant our Confession of Faith, the good old ways of worship will be forsaken for unscriptural innovations, and the tinsel of a superficial religiousness will take the place of genuine godliness." Whatever God may do in His sovereignty with the truth amidst error His blessing cannot be expected upon preaching and practice which go contrary to His Word.

Bonar, who was obviously sensitive to the thrust of Kennedy's arguments, does not seriously deal with the doctrinal and practical issues on which Kennedy focuses but majors on personalities and on perceived cultural differences between the north and south of Scotland as the reason for Kennedy's disapproval of Moody and those supporting him. Kennedy is not distracted and his *Reply* elucidates even more clearly the fundamental flaws of the new evangelicalism. He calls readers who endorsed preaching which marginalised the law, the fact and implications of man's depravity, the necessity of the new birth which precedes any human movement Godwards and the sovereignty of God in the dispensing of Grace, back to the preaching of Jesus in John 6 as a model Gospel sermon. In so doing he makes many perceptive and thought provoking observations on themes basic to the Gospel and its preaching such as the necessary use of the law, the danger of substituting faith for Christ and of making faith nothing more than a natural belief and making assurance nothing more than the awareness that one has this belief. He also discusses the basis on which, and the terms in which, the Gospel is preached to all.

The ultimate test of who was right in this argument is the Word of God, and this republication will justify itself if it constrains readers to subject their beliefs and practices to Biblical scrutiny. History confirms the accuracy of Kennedy's Biblical assessment in that it reveals the impetus given by Moody's campaign to the departure of the Scottish Churches from Biblical doctrine and practice and reveals the shallowness and barrenness characteristic of Scottish Church life on the whole during the subsequent 120 years. We must apply the same tests to every attempt to make the Gospel relevant and be resolved, in the spirit of the Gospel, to adhere to the doctrines and practices of the Word, looking for blessing to the Sovereign Lord whose prerogative it is to bless.

Hugh M. Cartwright
Edinburgh, 6 December, 1996.

Part One:

HYPER-EVANGELISM

JOHN KENNEDY

HYPER-EVANGELISM

'ANOTHER GOSPEL,' THOUGH A MIGHTY POWER.

A REVIEW

OF THE

RECENT RELIGIOUS MOVEMENT IN SCOTLAND

BY

J. KENNEDY, D.D.
DINGWALL.

SEVENTH EDITION.

EDINBURGH:
DUNCAN GRANT & COMPANY,
FORREST ROAD.
1874.

PRICE SIXPENCE.

HYPER-EVANGELISM

WHEN a movement is in progress in our land, during which many are awakened to thought and feeling as to eternal things, who were utterly unthinking and insensate before, when thousands think that they have lately believed in Christ, and with the joy of assurance profess that they have found Him, when from the church are seen issuing many, who have enlisted as recruits, in a crusade against the ungodliness and unbelief of the world, when so many, who have a high position and commanding influence in the church, declare that it is a gracious work of God by which these results have been produced, and when many more, believing this, are exceeding glad and abound in thanksgiving, sad, yea, strained to breaking, must be the heart of one, who seeks the glory of God and the salvation of souls, if he cannot share in the prevalent hopefulness and joy. Being one of those, to whom the present movement has hitherto yielded more grief than gladness, I feel constrained to tell why I am a mourner and apart.

PRELIMINARY REMARKS

1. Those who, ere the movement had been developed into its abiding fruits, hastened to declare it to be a gracious work of God, must have laid claim to inspiration; and only if that claim is good can their judging be allowable. It may be legitimate to form an *unfavourable* judgment, even at the outset of a religious awakening, if the means employed in producing it are such as the Lord cannot be expected to bless; but a *favourable* verdict at that stage, no man, not a prophet, has any right to pronounce.

Only He who "trieth the hearts and reins" can then judge. He allows His disciples to try to know men only by their fruits (Matt. 7:20). Not at the outset, and not by the immediate results, but by the fruits produced after trial, does He allow them to form a favourable judgment regarding a religious movement (John 8:31). It is not enough to justify such a verdict, that souls are anxious, that anxious souls attain to a faith that is assured, and to a joy that is exceeding, and that a change of conduct and zealous service are for a season the result. All this was, once and again, under the ministry of Jesus Himself, without any lasting and saving result; and men are sadly forgetful and madly bold, who in the face of such a fact venture to trace similar ap-

13

pearances at once to a gracious work of God (John 6, 8, 12).

2. One is not compelled to affirm that a religious movement is not a work of grace, if he refrains from saying that it is. This is a position into which some men, more zealous than discerning, seek to drive those who do not share their own blind sanguineness. I am not to judge, at the outset, except of the means employed, and if these are unscriptural, I am forbidden to expect a good result (Isa. 8:20). If the means employed and the agents are unexceptionable, I can legitimately form no decided opinion of the work, till its fruits are in due time developed.

3. There is no necessity for regarding it as the great Deceiver's work, if it is considered not to be a gracious work of God. There are impressions, which are not saving, produced by Divine influence in connection with the gospel (Heb. 6:4-6). The temporary impressions produced by the preaching of Christ are instances of this. But that Satan can produce counterfeit, as surely as the Lord can make real, converts, I firmly believe. And when he is at work, as "an angel of light," he best succeeds when men blindly accept, instead of wisely testing, the results. There is, surely, some reason to fear that his hand is on the agents as well as on the subjects of the work, when neither are careful to apply the test of truth (John 3:20,21; 1 John 4:1).

4. If I regard with little hopefulness a movement over which so many are chanting songs of joy, till all Christendom bends its ear to the voice of gladness that thrills from our land, my saying so will suffice to make some men decry me as opposed to a revival of the work of the Lord. To this I lay my account. If the Lord knows that I am not, I feel not very anxious as to the judgment of men. But which of us incurs the greater responsibility, you, who proclaim this movement to be a work of grace, or I, who cannot say that I as yet do so regard it? You commit the credit of true religion to cases which have not been proved—you point the attention of the ungodly to individuals whom you declare to be converts, and you call on them to judge of godliness by these; you tell those, who are suddenly impressed, that they have been born again, when you know not whether they were or not; you tell the Church to count on a great accession to her strength, when, so far as you can know, only traitors may be added to her ranks; you say, with the voice of thanksgiving to God, that He has done a work which you cannot know that He will acknowledge to be His. Yours, at any rate, is a tremendous responsibility. And if your estimate is false— and you cannot as yet possibly prove it to be true—how fearful the results must be! You will have hardened in ungodliness an unbelieving world; you will have flattered into delusive security precious perishing souls; you will have cheated the Church by inducing her to form a false estimate of her strength; and you will have dishonoured God by ascribing to Him work which his hand had never wrought. I merely refrain from judging anything "before the time." What I judge now, I am required to judge. I form an opinion, as one bound to "try the spirits" of the doctrines and modes of service which are the means of advancing the movement. If I do so fairly, I am so far free from blame. If my estimate is proved to be false as well as unfavourable, I am guilty, and if I formed it under the influence of prejudice, I am very guilty; I suffer in the lack of the hope and gladness by which the hearts of others are so greatly stirred; and I incur a woe, if, under the influence of a biased opinion of the work, I refuse to take part in it, though called to do so by the Lord (Judges 5:23).

5. Of the means employed in promoting such a work, one is bound to judge. I am not to be blinded by dazzling results. A worthy end does not sanctify all the means that may be used in attaining it, nor does a seemingly good result justify all the means employed in producing it. Many seem to think that if they choose to call a religious movement a work of grace, no fault should be found with any instrumentality employed in advancing it. All must be right, they think, if the result is to be regarded as a revival of the work of God. To censure any doctrine preached, or any mode of worship practised, seems to them to be opposition to the good work, and to tend to mar its progress. They may be of the same opinion, as to the impropriety of some of the means which are employed, with those who do not refrain from condemning them, but for the work's sake they tolerate them. As if the Lord's work could receive aid from aught that was unscriptural! An enemy's hand is surely here. May it not be, that under cover such as this, the deceiver is introducing into the creed and worship of the Church what shall be statedly obstructive to a real work of grace? Some there are who have this fear. It were well if all were careful lest this should be the result of acquiescence in unscriptural teaching and practices.

6. Some ministers, who took part with hesitation in the movement, justify their having done so by declaring their object to have been to check irregular tendencies, and to shape the development of the work. And what has been the issue of their prudence? They merely served to swell the volume, while utterly powerless to control the force, of the current. Hundreds of ministers have I seen, sitting as disciples at the feet of one whose teaching only showed his ignorance even of "the principles of the doctrine of Christ;" who, to their face, called the church-es, which they represented, "first-class mobs;" was organising before their eyes an association, for religious objects, outside the churches, which may yet prove as troublesome as the naked forces of the world; was casting ridicule on their old forms of worship, which they were sworn to uphold; and was proposing to convert prayer-meetings into occasions of religious amusement, a change which he certainly did not ask them to approve, without giving them a specimen, which excited the laughter of thousands, and gave to themselves a sensation of merry-making in the house of the Lord.

7. I carefully refrain from forming an estimate of the results of this work, as these are to be found in individual cases. I confine myself to the general character of the movement, in so far as that is determined by the more prominent teaching under which it has advanced, and in connection with its bearing on the religious condition of the country. I most persistently continue to hope that good has been done; for even were I persuaded that Satan was busy in forging counterfeits, I can-not conceive what would induce him to do so, unless he was provoked by a genuine work of grace which he was anxious to discredit and to mar.

There are two reasons why I cannot regard the present religious movement hopefully. 1. Because the doctrine which is the means of impression seems to me to be "another gospel," though a mighty in-fluence. Hyper-Evangelism I call it, because of the loud professions of evangelism made by those who preach it; and because it is just an ex-treme application of some truths, to the neglect of others which are equally important parts of the great system of evangelic doctrine. 2. Because unscriptural practices are resorted to in order to advance the movement.

HYPER-EVANGELISM "ANOTHER GOSPEL"

IN forming an estimate of the doctrine that was mainly effective in advancing the movement, I had sufficient materials at hand. I heard the leading teacher repeatedly, and I perused with care published specimens of his addresses. I have before me as I write what appears to me amply to justify all that I venture to affirm. Those who were present to hear, will recollect enough to enable them to judge of the correctness of my account of the kind of instruction by which such marked and frequent impressions were produced.

My objection, to the teaching to which I refer, is, that it ignores the supreme end of the gospel which is the manifestation of the Divine glory; and misrepresents it as merely unfolding a scheme of salvation adapted to man's convenience. It drops the first note of the angel's song, in which the gospel is described as "glory to God in the highest, and on earth peace, good will toward men." This objection has grown and been confirmed in my mind, by considering, 1. That no pains are taken to present the character and claims of God as Lawgiver and Judge, and no indication given of a desire to bring souls, in self-condemnation, to "accept the punishment of their iniquity." 2. That it ignores the sovereignty and power of God in the dispensation of His grace. 3. That it affords no help to discover, in the light of the doctrine of the cross, how God is glorified in the salvation of the sinner that believeth in Jesus. 4. That it offers no precaution against tendencies to antinomianism on the part of those who profess to have believed.

1. *No pains are taken to present the character and claims of God as Lawgiver and Judge, and no indication given of a desire to bring souls in self-condemnation, to accept the punishment of their iniquity.*

The law of God has its place in the book, and its use in the work of God. "By the law is the knowledge of sin;" and the Spirit, who convinces of sin, uses it in that department of His work. A due regard to the glory of God demands that it be so used. Sinners are not to be saved on a misunderstanding as to what they are, and as to what they merit. They must know Him against whom they have sinned. They must know what is justly due to Him from them as His creatures. They must be made acquainted with their iniquity as well as guilt, as

17

sinners. And through the coming of the commandment sin must "revive" in their consciousness, so that they shall know that their hearts are desperately wicked, as surely as that their persons are condemned to die. *Without this they can have no conception of gospel grace.* Any hope attained to without this, can only be based on a misunderstanding, and must involve dishonour to God. God is not to be conceived of as one who has to study man's convenience only, instead of supremely consulting His own glory. It should be an aim of preaching, therefore, to bring sinners to plead guilty before God; to feel themselves, in excuseless guilt, shut up to the sovereign mercy of Him against whom they have sinned. The attainment of this may be the result of a moment's working of the power of God, or it may be reached only after a protracted process; but to this all must come who are reconciled to God.

True, it cannot be expected that the operation of the applied law, on an unrenewed soul, can ever bring him to submit to God's claims as a Lawgiver, or to His terms as a Saviour. Subjection of the will to the law, is as impossible as submission to "the righteousness of God," on the part of an unregenerate sinner.

And this is one reason why this is not insisted on in ultra-evangelic teaching. To insist on God's claims,—to consider what is due to God in the personal transaction between the sinner and Him as to peace,—would bring the moral as well as the legal difficulty into view, and thus the necessity of the new birth would have to be faced as well as that of atonement. The latter cannot be passed over by any who profess to preach the gospel at all, though in the teaching referred to it is most perfunctorily dealt with; but the former, as shutting up souls to repentance, to which only the renewed can attain, is most persistently ignored.

And this is done professedly in the interest of gospel grace. To require men to consider the claims of God as Lawgiver and Judge, in order that they may feel themselves shut up to His mercy as Sovereign, seems to such teachers to be raising an obstruction between sinners and the grace of the gospel. It seems hard to them that man's convenience should be interfered with by the claims of God. A call to repentance, therefore, never issues from their trumpet. In their view, there is no place for repentance either before or after conversion. A vague, brief sense of danger is all that is required at the outset; and converts are taught that, once they have believed, they are not to remember and mourn for their sins. "Why raise up your sins again, to think of and to confess them?" their leading teacher said to them; "for were they not disposed of nearly two thousand years ago? Just believe this, and go home, and sing, and dance." It is no wonder, then, that they decry as not evangelical the preaching that does not ignore repentance. But they forget that, on the same ground, they might bring this charge against the Word of God itself; and not only against the Book of Exodus, but against the Epistle to the Romans as well, the writer of which had not learned how to bring men to know the grace of the gospel, except by bringing them first to know God and His law, their sin and its demerit, and their hearts and their desperate wickedness. What a strange delusion men labour under who imagine that what is essential to any right appreciation of the grace of God and to an intelligent submission to it, must be dispensed with, in order to guard the freeness of the gospel! By a "free gospel" they can only intend to indicate a gospel that suits a sinner's disposition, instead of being adapted to his state, that dispenses with all humbling of the soul before God, and of which man, unaided, can make use. Verily, for the defence of such a gospel, repentance must be excluded.

The favourite doctrine of sudden conversion is practically a complete evasion of the necessity of repentance. Suddenness is regarded as the rule, and not the exception, in order to get rid of any process preliminary to faith. And on what ground do they establish this rule? Merely on the instances of sudden conversion recorded in Scripture. True, there are cases not a few of sudden conversion recorded in Scripture, and there have been such instances since the Book of God was sealed. There was a wise and gracious design in making them thus marked at the outset. They were intended, by their extraordinary suddenness, to show to all ages the wondrous power of God. But was their suddenness designed to indicate the rule of God's acting in all ages? This it will be as difficult to establish, as that the miraculous circumstances attending some of them were intended to be perpetual. The work of conversion includes what we might expect to find detailed in a process. There can be no faith in Christ without some sense of sin, some knowledge of Christ, such as never was possessed before, and willingness, resulting from renewal, to receive Him as a Saviour from sin. If a hearty, intelligent turning to God in Christ be the result of conversion, it is utterly unwarrantable to expect that, as a rule, conversion shall be sudden. Indeed, the suddenness is rather a ground of suspicion than a reason for concluding that the work is God's. The teaching of Christ, in the parable of the sower, warrants this suspicion. They who are represented as suddenly receiving the word with joy are those who, in time of temptation, fall away. Suddenness and superficiality are there associated, and with both ephemeralness. In the experience of some, whose conversion was sudden, there was, as in the case of the great Apostle of the Gentiles, an after-process, intended to prepare them for useful service in the church. And is it not the fact, that those, who were most remarkable, in later times, for their godliness and their usefulness, were the subjects of a detailed and extended process, before attaining to "peace and joy in believing?"

The extremely unguarded use of the statement, that it is through faith, and not through feeling, salvation is attained, tends to the same effect. True, there is a danger of hampering oneself by the idea that, unless there is a certain state of conscious feeling, an effort to believe is vain. There is a danger, too, of substituting feeling for faith, and of resting on a certain experience, instead of on what is objectively presented in the Word, as a ground of hope. All earnest souls are apt, at a certain stage, to search for the warrant of faith in their own state of feeling, rather than in the written Word. True, reception of Christ is the immediate duty of all who hear the gospel; and nought can excuse their not doing so. But is it not extremely dangerous even to appear to say that faith is the opposite of feeling? Does not faith itself express a state of feeling? Is it not an exercise of the heart as well as of the understanding? Those who so thoroughly separate faith and feeling, are led to regard faith as merely the assent of the understanding to certain statements regarding the way of salvation. And is it not the practice of some evangelists to press men to believe certain propositions, while telling them that their state of feeling is to be made no account of, that they are just to receive these as true, and that, if they do so, they are to regard that belief as faith, and at once to conclude that they are saved because they have so believed. It seems to be imagined that, in order to have in faith the opposite of works, it is necessary to reduce it to mere belief. But in reality this is but to place it on the same footing with works. Faith, as mere belief, is considered to be something within the power of all; and, by reducing it to a minimum of effort, both as to time and action, it is made to appear to be something different from protracted self-righteous labour. *But it is only different as an easier thing for men to do.* Never can faith be truly seen to be opposed to works, till it is considered as indicating a state of feeling,—till it is seen to be a "believing with the heart;" for it is only when it is regarded as a hearty reception of Christ Himself as "all in all," that salvation through faith can be recognised as salvation by grace. To some minds the facility and the suddenness seem essential to the graciousness of faith. They reduce it to mere belief, that men may appear able to do it, and it must be done at once, that there may be no room for repentance, and that it may appear to be something else than a work. *But there never was more legal doctrine delivered, than that of those, who urge men to mere belief, in order to salvation.*

2. It ignores the sovereignty and power of God in the dispensation of His grace.

This omission is usually justified on the ground, that references to these are apt to be abused or to give needless offence. If men are to be told that salvation is entirely at the disposal of God's sovereign will, and that sinners are so utterly lost that only the working of God's power can move them, either to will or to do, what is required by the claims of the law and by the call of the gospel, then the result will be, that some will be offended and go away, others fold their hands and sleep, and others still sink down into despair. Am I therefore to refrain from proclaiming Jehovah as King? Am I to be silenced by fear of the result of telling, that it is His right to regulate, by His own sovereign will, His own work of grace? Am I not rather very specially called to announce His sovereignty in connection with salvation? In no other sphere does he appear more gloriously kingly than in this. Did not the Divine preacher make the sovereignty of God the theme of His very first sermon, though His hearers were thereby so incensed, that only by a miracle could He preserve His life from their fury? (Luke 4). And did He not, in all His preaching, ascribe salvation to the sovereign will of the Father who sent Him?

Men, anxious to secure a certain result, and determined to produce it, do not like to think of a controlling will, to whose sovereign behests they must submit, and of the necessity of almighty power being at work, whose action must be regulated by another will than theirs. Certain processes must lead to certain results. This selfish earnestness, this proud resolve to make a manageable business of conversion-work, is intolerant of any recognition of the sovereignty of God. "Go to the street," said the great American evangelist, to a group of young ladies, who were seated before him, "and lay your hand on the shoulder of every drunkard you meet, and tell him that God loves him, and that Christ died for him; and *if you do so, I see no reason why there should be an unconverted drunkard in Edinburgh for forty-eight hours.*"

There is of course frequent reference to the Spirit, and an acknowledgment of the necessity of His work, but there is, after all, very little allowed to Him to do; and bustling men feel and act as if somehow His power was under their control. There is a prevalent notion, only in a few utterances assuming definite shape, that there is a pervading gracious presence of the Holy Spirit, requiring only, in order to its effective influence, a certain state of feeling and a certain amount of effort. There is prayer, but many who engage in it look around them for an overflowing, rather than upward for an outpouring, of the Spirit of promise. There is prayer, but it is rather to constitute a ground of hope, than the result of reaching that which is set before us in the gospel. Faith in the efficacy of prayer is far more common than faith in the Hearer of prayer. *Prayer, in order to produce expectation, may seem to be followed by an answer, when the susceptibility, caused by the hopefulness it engendered, accounts for all the result.*

It is true, that it is quite as unwarrantable, to expect the outpouring of the Spirit, without prayer for His coming, as it is to hope for His coming because this has been asked. There is a call and encouragement to ask, and those who ask in faith shall never ask in vain; but the asking is under the sovereign control of God as surely as the giving. I believe, too, that men professing to ask for the coming of the Comforter, may really be asking something else, and may, in answer to their cry, be receiving as a judgment what they regard as a mercy. It is also true that, to pray for the Spirit's coming, and not to employ, in all earnestness, the means which He has been wont to acknowledge and to use, is nothing short of presumption. To wait for His coming is not to be idle till He comes. But it is also true, that those, who are blindly craving some excitement, may be preparing instruments to be used by some other power than that of the Spirit of the Lord. The prayers and the efforts, the asking and the preparation, may correspond, but the one may be directed towards something else than that which is presented in the promise of the Lord, and the other adapted for another hand than that by which the promise is fulfilled. It is true, besides, that the withholding of the Spirit, in His gracious influences, is a token of the Lord's anger provoked by iniquity, but it is terrible to think of an impenitent people, regarding as a gracious work of God that which is really not so, that, under covert of an imagined mercy, they may remain at ease in their sins, and congratulate themselves on having been favoured by the Lord, without having to part with their idols.

In the present movement, at any rate, there seems to be little that is allowed of work to the Spirit of the Lord. In the prominent teaching, there is no exposure of the total depravity and the utter spiritual impotence of souls "dead in trespasses and sins." To face this reality in the light of God's word, would be to discover the necessity of the Almighty agency of the Holy Ghost. This cannot be endured. But another reason must be assigned for avoiding the doctrine of total depravity. To preach it is decried as treating men as inert matter, to be wrought upon, but never to be active. This must not be preached to sinners, it is said, lest they fold their hands and sleep. They are intelligent and responsible beings, and must be differently dealt with. And how do you propose to treat them? *Are you to hide from them what they must know, ere they can ever act as intelligent beings in dealing with their souls' condition?* Are you to set them to work, as if they were what they are not? Is this your way of urging them to act as becomes responsible beings? You would hoodwink their understandings, and misdirect the movements to which their sense of responsibility urges them! But you hide the true state of things from yourselves as well as from them. You do so that you may have hope of success. You have no faith in the Spirit as God. You cannot bear, therefore, to discover that there is a great work for Him to do; and you cannot endure to feel dependent on His love, for you cannot trust in it as the love of God; and if you think of it as Divine, you know that you must also think of it as sovereign. And you would fain account the work to be done as not too much for your own power of persuasion; for you are ambitious of having it to do yourselves, as well as hopeless of having it done by the Lord. And yet, forsooth, you are the men who have faith, and those who differ from you are the dupes of unbelief. Yes, you are men of faith, but yours is faith in men. The man who can cry in faith for life, with a valley of dry bones before him, is the man who has faith in God.

Sometimes, an address may be heard, in which the necessity of regeneration is very strongly urged, but this is sure to be followed by some statement that blunts the edge of all that was said before. After some strong sayings about the necessity of regeneration, in one of the leader's addresses, the question was put, "How is this change to be attained?" And the speaker answered the question by saying, "You believe, and then you are regenerated;" and in confirmation, he referred to John 1:12, forgetting the verse which follows! Faith regenerates! If it does so, as the act of a living soul, then the soul could not have been dead in sins. If it was, whence came the life put forth in believing? If that regenerating faith was the act of a dead soul, then a dead man, by his own act, brings himself alive! The same teacher said on another occasion, "God would not call men to believe, unless they had the power to do so." I would like to hear his answer to the question,

Can natural men "love God with all their heart, and soul, and mind, and strength," who yet are required by God to do so? And how would he expound the words, "The natural man receiveth not the things of the Spirit of God; for they are foolishness unto him; neither can he know them, because they are spiritually discerned;" and the words of Jesus, "No man can come unto me, except the Father who hath sent me, draw him."

There is a faith which can be exercised without the gracious aid of the Holy Ghost, but it cannot be the faith that is "to the saving of the soul." That is expressly declared to be "of the operation of God," and to require for its production "the working of His mighty power which He wrought in Christ, when He raised Him from the dead." *That faith stakes the eternal all of an immortal being, who is a lost sinner, on the truth of Divine testimony.* Can one do so who does not regard the testimony as Divine? Can one so regard it who does not realise that God is, and that He speaks in that testimony to him? Can a dead soul thus believe? As well expect a sense of your presence, and a response to your words, from the bones that lie mouldering in the grave, beside which you stand and speak. True, there may be a persuasion of the truth, arising from its correspondence to the dictates of conscience, and because of evidence which has led to a rational conviction of its divinity; for in the grave, in which lie the spiritually dead, there is still intellectual life and a moral faculty that may occasionally be very active. But this is something very different from the faith in God, which is the gift of God. *That faith, too, respects the person of Christ.* It does so, not merely as looking to the historical personage who appears in the inspired record, nearly two thousand years apart, in the hazy past from us, who has left a gospel and a salvation with us, with which, apart from His person, we can deal by faith. It not only realises Jesus of Nazareth as the Christ and the Son of God, but it apprehends Him as a living present Saviour in the testimony of God regarding Him. It actually receives Him as He is actually presented by God. It embraces Himself in order to finding all in Him. It is not merely belief in testimony, it is also trust in the person who is presented therein. It is the homage of confidence in and submission to the Son of God as Jesus the Christ of God. *That faith, besides, implies unreserved dependence on the grace of God.* It is not merely taking advantage of a convenient ground of hope. It is an acknowledgment, at the footstool of the Divine throne, of being justly condemned and of being utterly helpless,—it is the acceptance of salvation from the hands of the Sovereign in order "to the praise of His grace." *That faith is, moreover, the cordial re-*

ception of Christ in order to salvation from all sin. It is not the mere appropriation of the boon of deliverance from death. This is all that is desired by those, who allow themselves to be hurried vaguely to believe in the love of God, and the substitutionary death of Jesus. True faith is the act of a soul who, up to that hour, was a lover of sin and an enemy to holiness, but who now cordially receives the Saviour in order to the destruction of what he loved, and to the attainment of what he hated before. Can a man thus believe who has not been regenerated by the Holy Ghost? And why hide from sinners that they cannot? Surely this cannot be wisely done in order to make gospel grace more manifest. Which knows best about the grace of the gospel, the man who thinks he is saved by grace through a faith which he owes to himself alone, or the man who has also learned that the faith, through which he is saved, is not of himself, but "is the gift of God"? Did Jesus hide this in His preaching from His hearers? Did He do so in His first sermon (Luke 4)? Did He do so in His first recorded dealing with an inquirer (John 3)? Did He not openly proclaim this in His great gospel sermon addressed to a multitude by the sea of Galilee (John 6)? It was while preaching that sermon He said, "No man can come unto me except the Father, which hath sent me, draw him."

It does raise one's indignation to hear some men speak of what would conserve, to the Spirit of God, His place and His work, as a mere obscuration of the grace of the gospel, and a fettering of souls in bondage. But it grieves one's heart to know that this is tolerated, and even approved of, by some who ought to be more zealous, for the grace and glory of the Lord, than to be able to endure it.

3. *No care is taken to show, in the light of the doctrine of the cross, how God is glorified in the salvation of a sinner.*

The designed overliness with which the doctrine of sin is stated, necessarily leads to this. The omission of any definite unfolding of the law's claims, and of any distinct tracing of the sinner's relation to it and to God—the lack of all that would raise the question, "How can God be just in justifying the ungodly?"—leaves the anxious in such a state of mind and feeling, that all they require, to satisfy them, is to discover that they have a convenient warrant to hope. Neither teacher nor disciple seems to desiderate aught besides the assurance, that salvation can be reached through faith. The gospel seems convenient for man, and that suffices. How salvation is to the praise of God's glory the one is not careful to show, the other is not anxious to know. To any unprejudiced observer, this must have appeared a marked feature

25

of revival teaching.

True, much use is made of Christ's substitutionary death. But it is usually referred to only as disposing of sin, so that it no longer endangers him, who believes that Christ died for him—who accepts Christ as his substitute. This use of the doctrine of substitution has been very frequent and very effective. Christ, as the substitute of sinners, is declared to be the object of faith. But it is His substitution rather than Himself. To believe in the substitution is what produces the peace. This serves to remove the sense of danger. There is no direct dealing with the person who was the substitute. There is no appreciation of the merit of His sacrifice, because of the Divine glory of Him by whom it was offered. Faith, in the convenient arrangement for deliverance from danger, is substituted for trust in the Person who glorified God on the earth, and "in whom" alone we can "have redemption through His blood." The blood of Jesus was referred to, and there was an oft-repeated "Bible-reading" on the subject of "the blood;" but what approximation to any right idea regarding it could there be in the mind, and what but misleading in the teaching, of one who could say, "Jesus left His blood on earth to cleanse you, but He brought His flesh and bones to heaven."

Souls who have a vague sense of danger, excited by the sensational, instead of an intelligent conviction of sin, produced by the light and power of applied truth, are quite ready to be satisfied with such teaching as this. To these, such doctrine will bring all the peace they are anxious to obtain. But what is the value of that peace? It is no more than the quiet of a dead soul, from whom has been removed an unintelligent sense of danger. A true sense of peace with God there cannot be, unless a sinner, assured that God was glorified by Him who died on the cross, can, with reverence of His glorious name, approach Him in the right of the crucified and exalted Jesus, having hope of acceptance in His sight. To this he cannot attain till, in the light of the Son's glory, he appreciates the merit of Jesus' blood, comes to Christ Himself to appropriate His blood in Him, approaches through Him to God, and receives, by the application of the promise of peace, a persuasion of acceptance, in faith, from the throne.

Where there is no wounding, there can be no healing, of conscience. The doctrine, that can do neither, can only do deceiver's work. A sinner, having peace without knowing, or caring to know, how the law, which he has transgressed, hath been magnified, how the justice, that demanded his death, hath been satisfied, how the name of God, which was by him dishonoured, has by Christ been glorified, and how what availed for these ends can be a ground of hope to him, in the presence of the God with whom he hath to do, may have enjoyment, may be zealous, may be active, but cannot have "a good hope through grace."

4. No precaution is offered against a tendency to antinomianism in those who profess to have believed.

Yea, this tendency must be fostered by the teaching given to them. If the law of God has not its own place accorded to it, in connection with the sinner's natural relation to God, and in order to conviction of sin, it is not likely to get it at a later stage. The man, who is disposed to think of his sin, as a great calamity, rather than as a heinous crime, is not likely either to reverence God or to respect His law. To his view, salvation is something which it would not be fair to withhold from him, rather than a gracious gift which a sovereign God is glorified in bestowing. The government under which he ventures to claim his salvation presents nothing venerable to his mind. He thinks of an easy reign of mercy, under which he can be as imperious as if his own will were law. In his altered position, it is easy for him to ignore the law of God. He never had to face it; and, if he has faith without life, there is nothing in him to incline him to do so now. Not having respect to the standard of God's law, it is easy for him to imagine that he is without sin. He is taught that now he has nothing to do with confession of sin, because his sins were long ago disposed of, and that he should not now remember them. As for "the corruption of his whole nature," it never was a trouble to him, and is less likely to be so now than before, since a delusive peace has drugged his soul to sleep. Antinomianism leading, in the first instance, to perfectionism, must be the result of the teaching under which he has been trained. In his leader's prayers he never hears any confession of sin, and he is apt to think that, if he follows him, he must be right. True, he is urged to work; and there is no service, however high, which, during his noviciate, he is not directed to attempt. The work which he is disposed to choose, and the first work he is instructed to engage in, is to preach to others what he himself has found. Meetings are multiplied that he may attend them, and crowds are gathered that he may address them. The excitement of his first impressions is thus to be kept up by the bustle of evangelistic service. And what kind of being is he likely to become under such training as this? A molluscous, flabby creature, without pith or symmetry, breathing freely only in the heated air of meetings, craving to be pampered with vapid sentiment, and so puffed up by foolish flattery, as to be in a state of chronic flatulency, requiring relief in frequent bursts of hymn-singing, in spouting addresses as void of Scripture truth as of common sense, and in belching flippant questions in the face of all he meets. Self-examination he discards as a torture only meant for slaves, humility and watchfulness as troublesome virtues which the wise will eschew, secret communion with God as a relic of less enlightened and less busy times, and the quiet habitual discharge of home duties, in the fear of God, as a tame routine for legalists.

The doctrine of assurance, which is preached, tends to the same effect. Assurance is regarded as the direct result of faith, or as essential to its exercise. A consciousness of faith is of itself deemed a sufficient ground of assurance. There is no place at all allowed to an attestation of faith by works. True, faith does often rise into assurance as to the sufficiency of Christ, as its object, and of the Word of God, as its warrant. There is a hope arising from the consciousness of this faith, as well as a hope occasioned by its exercise. But there is also a place reserved by God for the hope arising from the attestation of faith by works. And the Lord calls the believer to examine himself, as to the fruits which his faith produceth, in order to ascertain that his faith is genuine, and that therefore Christ is already his. "Faith without works is dead." Where there is a careful disallowing of self-examination, there is sufficient proof of the law being ignored, as the authoritative rule of the Christian's life. Suggestions, to this exercise, are not infrequently decried as temptations of Satan, or as necessarily the result of backsliding. And why so? Because it is imagined, that a man is not required to prove himself to be a genuine believer, by doing the will of Christ, in obedience to His law. And yet it will be on the ground of works, as evidence of true faith, that Christ Himself, on His great white throne, will justify the verdict which proclaims them blessed, who are heirs of the kingdom, prepared by His Father.

A religion without reverence and without contrition, can alone be fostered under such teaching as this. But now, as surely as of old, "Thus saith the Lord," "To this man will I look, even to him that is poor, and of a contrite spirit, and trembleth at my word." Now, as of old, the heirs of the "kingdom which cannot be moved," "serve God acceptably with reverence and godly fear"; and only in that measure can they taste "the peace of God," and "rejoice with joy unspeakable and full of glory."

HYPER-EVANGELISM, A MIGHTY POWER

I MAKE no attempt to trace, to its source, the influence exerted in producing the marked effects resulting from the present religious movement. I confine my attention to the advantage, afforded by the state of feeling, which preceded that movement, and to certain elements of power in the means employed to advance it.

It was preceded by a very prevalent desire for a change. All classes of religious society seemed to be stirred by a wistful longing for something to break up the dead monotony, of which all were wearying. Some were actuated by genuine spiritual feeling. They felt that tokens of the Lord's absence abounded; and turning to the Lord they cried for the manifestation of His power and glory. Others, strangers to stated spiritual enjoyment in the means of grace, were longing for some change—some excitement to lift them out of their dullness—and for some bustle in which they might take their share of service. Others, still, who knew no happiness in the house of God, and had no desire for His presence, would fain that something new were introduced into the mode of service which they felt so jading. The excitement of a revival would be to them a relief. "Special services" they strongly craved. Prayer for a revival was called for; and many were ready to take part in the meetings convened for that purpose. These meetings resulted in the hope of an answer. Though but few truly appreciated what was needed, and really dealt with God, we cannot but hope that something was done by the Lord in answer to their cry. But many there were who merely craved a change,—something to relieve them of the tedium of a routine, in which they found no enjoyment, because they were estranged from God,—and who joined, in asking this, with those who were asking something better. These were the persons disposed to make much of their prayers, and who found it easy to hope just because they had chosen to ask; and they may have received, though not in mercy, what they sought. The expectation of a change, at any rate, was general. There was an opening up of men's minds to an expected influence. This tended to affect even the Gallios who "cared for none of those things." A revival was talked of, prayed for, and expected, and thus a general susceptibility of impression was produced. Prayer meetings, fostering the desire and expectation of a change, were in all places the pioneers of the movement. Those who heard that a revival had taken place elsewhere, sought that it might reach their own locality. Many blindly asked for what was done in other places, instead of seeking the fulfilment of the Lord's promise.

In course of time, musical practisings were added to prayer meetings, as preparation for a revival! From both the addresses and the music much was expected, when evangelistic deputies arrived.

What the effect would have been, had the awakened expectancy been left to be operated on by the stated ministrations of the sanctuary, or by extraordinary efforts, that introduced no departure from the usual mode of worship, no one can tell; but I cannot refrain from expressing my persuasion, that the result would have been a healthier one than that which new appliances developed.

But on this wakeful state of mind, was brought to bear, a system of doctrine, that ignored those aspects of the truth, which are most offensive to "the natural man," and that, while offering something that seemed plausible to an unenlightened conscience, seemed to conserve the old heart's imagined independence of the sovereign and almighty grace of God, and by ignoring repentance preserved to it its idols. The gospel, modified to suit the taste of unrenewed men, was welcome. The recommendations of it, given by men of influence, tended to put down suspicion, and to induce the public to receive it as "the gospel of the grace of God." The new style of teaching made it seem such an easy thing to be a Christian. To find oneself easily persuaded to believe what was presented as the gospel, and to think that by this faith salvation was secured, and that all cause of anxiety was for ever gone, gave a new and pleasing sensation, which thousands were willing to share.

And once the movement had begun it could command an indefinite supply of agents. All who say they were converted are set to work. Any one, who can tongue it deftly, can take a part,—he requires neither knowledge nor experience. The excitement is kept up by the bustle of public service. No fear is felt of lifting up novices "lest they fall into the condemnation of the devil." That feeling may have been suitable in Paul's day, but it has now ceased to be so regarded. But there is a fear of converts ceasing to seem to be so, if they are not kept busy in religious service. A proselytising bustle must therefore be the outcome of their faith. There is an utter avoidance of *testing* work on the part of their instructors; but *attesting* work enough is done. They have at once been proclaimed Christians in their own hearing, and in the presence of thousands; and those, who presume to tell them this, are quite ready to join with themselves in thinking that they are fit for any service that they may choose to try. A season apart, to be alone with God, a solemn time for careful counting of the cost, has from Christ the double recommendation of His example and of His precept, but is desired neither by nor for these so-called converts.

To these advantages for effect were added various devices, which, though quite unscriptural, or rather, because they were so, were fraught with impressing power.

UNSCRIPTURAL DEVICES

1. HYMN-SINGING

Excessive hymn-singing is one of these. The singing of uninspired hymns even in moderation, as a part of public worship, no one can prove to be scriptural; but the excess and the misdirection of the singing in this movement were irrational as well. Singing ought to be to the Lord; for singing is worship. But singing the gospel to men has taken the place of singing praise to God. This, at any rate, is something new—that indeed is its only recommendation—and when the singing is also good, its melody combines with its novelty to make an impression. The singing produced an effect. Many professed to have been converted by the hymns.

2. INSTRUMENTAL MUSIC

The use of instrumental music was an additional novelty, pleasing to the kind of feeling that finds pleasure in a concert. To introduce what is so gratifying there, into the service of the house of God, is to make the latter palatable to those to whom spiritual worship is an offence. The organ sounds effectively touch chords which nothing else would thrill. To Scottish Presbyterians it was something new; but as their spiritual guides did not object to it, why should they? Tided thus, by their pastors, over all difficulties, which their scruples might occasion, they found it pleasant to enjoy the new sensation. They could be at the concert and in church at the same time. They could get at once something for conscience and something for the flesh.

And yet it is not difficult to prove that the use of instrumental music, in the worship of God, is unscriptural, and that therefore all, who have subscribed the Confession of Faith, are under solemn vow against it. There was a thorough change, in the mode of worship, effected by the revolution, which introduced the New Testament dispensation. So thorough is this change, that no part of the old ritual can be a precedent to us. For all parts of the service of the house of God there must be New Testament precept or example. No one will pretend that for instrumental music, in the worship of God, there is any authority in New Testament Scripture. "The fruit of the lips," issuing from hearts that make "melody to the Lord," is the only form of praise it sanctions. The Church of Rome claims a right to introduce into the worship of God any innovation it lists; the Church of England allows what is not expressly forbidden in Scripture; but Scotch Presbyterians are bound, by the Confession of Faith, to disallow all that is not appointed in Scripture (Conf. chap. xxi.). How those, who allow the use of instrumental music, in our Assembly Hall, can reconcile their doing so with their ordination vows, I cannot even conjecture.

It may seem strange, but it is quite as true as it is strange, that those who are ready to plead that principles and doctrines, inculcated under the former dispensation, are no longer entitled to our acceptance, unless re-delivered with New Testament sanction, are just the parties who are also ready to go back to Old Testament antecedents in the mode of worship. What is eternally true is treated as if it were temporary, and that which has "vanished away" is regarded as perpetual. But if the ancient mode, of conducting the service of praise, furnishes an example for all times, on the self-same ground you are entitled to choose what you list out of the ceremonies of Old Testament worship. The altar and the sacrifice may be defended as surely as the organ.

"But we use the organ only as an aid," it is said. "It is right that we should do our best in serving the Lord; and if the vocal music is improved by the instrumental accompaniment, then surely the organ may be used." On the same ground you might argue for the use of crucifixes and pictures, and for all the paraphernalia of the Popish ritual. "These," you might say, "make an impression on minds that would not otherwise be at all affected. They vividly present before worshippers the scenes described in Scripture, and if, as aids, they serve to do so, they surely cannot be wrong." To this, there are three replies, equally good against the argument for instrumental music. **1.** They are not prescribed in New Testament Scripture, and therefore they must not be introduced into New Testament worship. **2.** They are incongruous with the spirituality of the New Testament dispensation. **3.** These additions but help to excite a state of feeling which militates against, instead of aiding, that which is produced by the word. An organ may make an impression, but what is it but such as may be made more thoroughly at the opera? It may help to regulate the singing, but does God require this improvement? And whence arises the taste for it? It cannot be from the desire to make the praise more fervent and spiritual, for it only tends to take attention away from the heart, whose melody the Lord requires. It is the craving for pleasurable aesthetics, for the gratification of mere carnal feeling, that desires the thrill of organ sounds, to touch pleasingly the heart, that yields no response to what is spiritual. If the argument, against the use of the organ, in the service of praise, is good, it is, at least, equally so against its use in the service of preaching. If anything did "vanish away," it surely is the use of all such accessories in connection with the exhibition of Christ to men.

3. THE INQUIRY ROOM

The novelty of the "inquiry room" was another effective aid in advancing this movement. It is declared to be desirable to come into close personal contact with the hearers of the gospel immediately after a sermon, in order to ascertain their state of feeling, to deepen impressions that may have been made, and to give a helping hand to the anxious. Such is the plea for "the inquiry room." In order that it may be supplied, hearers are strongly urged, after a sensational address, to take the position of converts or inquirers. They are pressed and hurried to a public confession. Strange means are resorted to, in order to commit them, by an open avowal of a certain state of feeling. But what right has any individual, not authorised by a Church of Christ, to do so,—to insist on a public confession on the part of any one? Even the Church can admit to a public confession only after trial. And the admission must be in connection with the dispensation of the appointed sealing ordinances. But here is a stranger, who never saw their faces before, hurrying people, whom a sensational address has excited, to make public profession of faith, thus associating them, without possibility of trial, with the Christians of the locality, and involving the credit of religion in their future conduct before the world. This, surely, is both unwise and presumptuous. How unlike this to the Divine Teacher's way! When a crowd of seemingly anxious souls gathered around Him, instead of urging them to confession, He tested them by searching doctrine, and the result was, that instead of crowding an inquiry room, they "went away and walked no more with Him." I feel persuaded that if an excited crowd, at a revival meeting, were to be addressed as were the multitude at the Sea of Galilee, the conductor would put the speaker down, denounce him for casting a gloom over the meeting, and give him no other opportunity of dealing with inquirers.

Why are men so anxious to keep the awakened in their own hands?

They, at any rate, seem to act as if conversion was all their own work. They began it, and they seem determined to finish it. If it is at all out of their hand, they seem to think that it will come to nothing. They must at once, and on the spot, get these inquirers persuaded to believe, and get them also to say that they do. They may fall to pieces if they are not braced round by a band of profession. Their names or number must, ere the night passes, be added to the roll of converts. They are gathered into the inquiry room, to act in a scene, that looks more like a part of a stage play, than aught more serious and solemn. Oh, what trifling with souls goes on in these inquiry rooms, as class after class is dealt with in rude haste, very often by teachers who never "knew the grace of God in truth!" The inquiry room may be effective in securing a hasty profession of faith, but it is not an institution which the Church of Christ should adopt or countenance.

4. OPEN PRAYER-MEETINGS

Even prayer-meetings are converted into factories of sensation. Brief prayers and brief addresses to the stroke of hammer, or the toll of bell, silent prayers, hymns, which often contain a considerable amount of nonsense, and occasionally of something worse, sung to the strains of an organ, and a chance to address or pray given to any one who chooses to rise and speak,—such are the arrangements of the new prayer-meeting. The *silent prayer*, what is it? It is secret prayer, and therefore ought to be prayer in secret. It must be *secret*, just because it is *silent*. And where is it engaged in? In the closet? No; it was Christ who directed it to be there. There are other leaders now, and they direct that it should be in open assembly. Christ would have men, when they pray secretly, to enter their closet and shut the door. Now it must be done so that those who do it "may be seen of men." And this device, so directly opposed to the mind of Christ, is lauded as if nothing could be better. And it is becoming the habit now of worshippers as they enter the house of God. They assume, before the eyes of hundreds, the attitude of prayer, to do, in the public assembly, what Christ directed to be done in the closet. If they intended this as a public confession of their sin, in neglecting prayer in their closet, such confession would not be at all uncalled for, if duly made. They who forget to do it where Christ required it to be done, are the persons most likely to do it where it can only be a bit of will-worship and formality.

The device of "open meetings," what of it? It is simply ceasing to take care that, in the worship of God, "all things be done decently and in order;" and giving the place to those who have conceit and tongue, and nought beside, which ought to be filled by those who in honour prefer others to themselves, and who seek grace to "serve with reverence and godly fear."

I have had to endure the trial of watching over a darling child, during her dying hours. Spasm, succeeding spasm, was the only movement indicating life, each one, as it came, shattering the frame which it convulsed, and thus wearing out its strength. While the spasms lasted I knew there still was life, but I also knew that these must soon end in death. There was life, but it was dying, and the convulsions of life soon ended in the stillness of death. But after the double pain came the ecstasy of a resurrection hope, and my heart could sing beside the grave, that covered for a season my dead out of sight. With still greater grief, should I look on my Church, in a spasmodic state, subject to convulsions, which only indicate that her life is departing, the result of revivals got up by men. It will be a sad day for our country, if the men, who luxuriate in the excitement of man-made revivals, shall, with their one-sided views of truth, which have ever been the germs of serious errors, their lack of spiritual discernment, and their superficial experience, become the leaders of religious thought, and the conductors of religious movements. Already they have advanced as many, as inclined to follow them, far in the way to Arminianism in doctrine, and to Plymouthism in service. They may be successful in galvanising, by a succession of sensational shocks, a multitude of dead, till they seem to be alive, and they may raise them from their crypts, to take a place amidst the living in the house of the Lord; but far better would it be to leave the dead in the place of the dead, and to prophesy to them there, till the living God Himself shall quicken them. For death will soon resume its sway. Stillness will follow the temporary bustle, and the quiet will be more painful than the stir. But to whatever extent this may be realised in the future of the Church in Scotland, our country shall yet share, in common with all lands, in the great spiritual resurrection that will be the morning work of that day of glory, during which "the knowledge of the Lord shall cover the earth," and "all nations shall be blessed in Messiah, and shall call Him blessed." Meantime, were it not for the hope of this, it would be impossible to endure to think of the present, and of the immediate future, of the cause of true religion in our land. The dead, oh, how dead! the living, oh, how undiscerning! And if there continue to be progress in the direction, in which present religious activity is moving, a negative theology will soon supplant our Confession of Faith, the good old ways of worship will be forsaken for unscriptural inventions, and the tinsel of a superficial religiousness will take the place of genuine godliness.

———————

Part Two:

THE OLD GOSPEL

HORATIUS BONAR

THE OLD GOSPEL:

NOT 'ANOTHER GOSPEL,'

BUT

THE POWER OF GOD UNTO SALVATION.

A REPLY TO DR. KENNEDY'S PAMPHLET, 'HYPER-EVANGELISM.'

By HORATIUS BONAR, D.D.

'THE FRUIT OF THE SPIRIT IS LOVE, JOY, PEACE, LONG-SUFFERING, GENTLENESS, GOODNESS, FAITH, MEEKNESS, TEMPERANCE.'—GAL. v.22.

EDINBURGH: ANDREW ELLIOT, 17 PRINCES STREET.
LONDON: JAMES NISBET AND CO.
1874.

PRICE EIGHTPENCE.]   [Fifth Thousand.

'Conscious of superiority, it is difficult for him to believe, that what he cannot appreciate can possibly be good. Men will try to form a positive judgment regarding all they think to be beneath themselves; and when they are compelled to feel that they cannot intelligently do so, they are very prone to vent their mortification in sweeping censures, or in expressions of contempt.'—DR. KENNEDY'S *Days of the Fathers in Ross-shire*, p. 79.

THE OLD GOSPEL

I REGRET both the tone and contents of this pamphlet. My regret concerning it is twofold. It condemns that which I believe to be a true work of God in our land, and it bears the honoured name of Dr. John Kennedy.

I write this reply to it in no unbrotherly spirit, but as one who, having had full knowledge of the work from the beginning, is not ashamed to bear his testimony concerning it; though in so doing he has to withstand a brother, and to say many things respecting his statements which he would gladly have left unsaid.

It is not the love of strife that draws me into the field. I have had enough of that in my day. The longer I live, the less I relish disputation among brethren; the more desirous I am to avoid giving offence; and to guard against uttering words that might only betray the wrath of man, or be the expression of self-will.

I write not so much in defence of brethren, as in vindication of the truth of God, and of the work of His Spirit; for I do not shrink from stating at the outset, that there is much in these strictures which appears to me at variance with the former, and in disparagement of the latter. If one brother, who has taken no part in this movement, steps forward either to question its value or to deny its divine origin, another brother, however inferior, who has had close, intimate, and continuous connection with it from the first, is warranted in taking up his pen to assert its worth, and speak out the strong conviction of his heart that it is thoroughly genuine, proceeding from the Holy Spirit,— a work not of man, but of God; not the product of excitement or religious panic, but the fruit of a soberly preached gospel; not the result of error, but of truth; not the beguilement of the impressible and unstable into a superficial and sentimental religiousness, but the winning of souls to God by the almighty power of the Spirit, through instruments which man may underrate, but which *God* has owned.

The knowledge which I have had of this work in all its parts from the beginning enables me to speak with some confidence. Dr. Kennedy has not had the opportunities which many, like myself, have had of witnessing all the various proceedings connected with it. He has not seen nor heard the hundredth part of what we have seen and heard. He has not come into close contact with the movement itself, nor into fellowship with the men who were its originators. He has not conversed personally with the hundreds of the awakened, as we have. He has not known the minor agents and agencies engaged in carrying on the movement. He has looked upon it from the outside, not from the inside; afar off, not near. He can only tell of what others have told him, not of what he has heard himself day by day for months. Almost all in this pamphlet is at second-hand; the statements of fact are only hearsay, such as no court of law, either civil or ecclesiastical, would sustain; nay, they consist of *anonymous hearsay,* the most unfair and suspicious kind of evidence, if it can be called evidence at all. Of legal and direct proof none is offered. The moral and indirect evidence comes to us in a very questionable shape, retailed at second-hand, coloured, shaped for the maintenance of a foregone conclusion, and affected (unconsciously, I believe) by a bias which makes it liable to suspicion throughout.

I confess I am surprised that one so skilful and so honourable as Dr. Kennedy should publish so many statements affecting the character of individuals *unauthenticated by a single name.* No witness is produced *in court,* and we are asked to believe one representation after another upon the *authority of nobody*. There is no signature to a single fact. Dr. Kennedy believes them, and vouches for them; that is all we know. *

---

* As Dr. Kennedy objects strongly to premature statements *in favour* of such a work, we might have expected him not to commit himself to premature conclusions *against it.* But he holds the somewhat peculiar opinion, that while we may pronounce an immediate judgment (as he has done) against it, no one ought to declare for it till after long probation. He would guard against premature conclusions on the one side, but not on the other! There is some singular bias here, as well as some defect in logic. It is affirmed that things are not ripe for a judgment in favour of the work, nor can be for years to come; but they are already ripe for a judgment against it. Well, if a judgment go against it now, and if it be a true one, it can never be reversed. The question cannot be re-opened, for the work has been authoritatively, and upon sufficient evidence, been declared to be *not* a work of God. Insufficient proof may be corroborated, and become sufficient; sufficient proof is incapable of becoming insufficient, as its very nature (sufficiency) excludes the possibility of reversal; so that no length of probation can ever show that to be a work of God which at the beginning was proved not to be so. Condemnation may be immediate, and it is irreversible; approbation must be the result of many years, and uncertain after all! This pamphlet ought, therefore, to have appeared ten months ago, if it was to do any good either to agents or converts. Mr. Moody should have been withstood at the time, not after he has left. The work should have been condemned last February, for the 'evil' was done before that.

Against no man are we entitled to receive an accusation, be it light or serious, save upon the testimony of competent and honest witnesses, 'purged of malice and partial counsel,' and openly adhibiting their names to the statements which they make, that men may form a calm and righteous judgment, according to the sufficiency of the evidence and the character of the witness. In the present pamphlet no witnesses are called, and no documents are produced. A full score of *unsupported* imputations are so made as to produce a most unfavourable impression in many ways against certain brethren; and yet the sources of information are so kept back, that no reader can verify these statements or test their exactness at any one point. The reports which have reached Dr. Kennedy may or may not be true. If he had appended the names of his witnesses, we should have been able to sift them for ourselves. He may have already sifted them, and given us, in this pamphlet, the results of that sifting. He does not say so. But even though he had thoroughly tested each one, still we should like to have the examination of the witnesses in our own hands, and to exercise the liberty of cross-questioning them.

Undoubtedly this pamphlet appeals to the Christian public of Scotland *as to a jury,* and the writer will be anxious to hear the judgment. But what honest jury will bring in a verdict of either guilty or not guilty, when the whole case presented to them turns upon second-hand and hearsay evidence; when not a single witness is produced in court, and there is only the prosecutor submitting his one-sided appeal, his coloured version of facts, and upon this, calling for a verdict in his favour, to the consternation of the honest twelve, who, after the opening statement, could not but expect to hear the names of the witnesses, and to obtain their evidence from their own lips, uncoloured by the prosecutor's bias?

It was this full probation that was gone about so manfully in the case of the Aberdeen awakening, under Mr. Burns, in the year 1841. The Presbytery took up the matter. There was a strong feeling manifested against the work and against Mr. Burns. The newspapers assailed both; and brethren in the Presbytery condemned both. Reports of the most unpleasant kind were circulated against the doctrine taught, and against the whole movement, as unscriptural and fanatical, as a thing of human excitement, carried on by suspicious methods, and certain to lead to the worst results. The *late* meetings were condemned; the *inquiry* meetings were specially denounced. The vehement addresses from the pulpit, and the earnest but sometimes abrupt way in which several of those engaged in the work appealed to individuals in private, and even in the streets, about the things of eternity; the peculiar and sometimes extreme ways in which truth was pressed upon the consciences either of the anxious or the unawakened,—these were things complained of, privately and publicly, in conversation and in the newspapers. Two classes objected: First, the worldly, who disliked all intensity of religious emotion. Then some hyper-Calvinistic brethren were alarmed at the fervent appeals of evangelists, who, perhaps, in the warmth of love for dying men, might have used indefensible expressions, and so incurred the displeasure of their calmer brethren, whose zeal for orthodoxy made a man an offender for a word, and who unfairly charged others with impugning or undermining doctrines which the accused held as honestly as the accusers. In short, the Aberdeen opposition to Mr. Burns and his work resembled in many aspects that which the present pamphlet exhibits. One Mr. Primrose, a good man, in his zeal for orthodoxy, could see nothing but evil in the movement. In his honest zeal, he held that 'it was not possible that the work in Aberdeen could be the work of God,' both because of the doctrine, and because of the screaming and sobbing and weeping and fainting which took place in the church.

Well, the Presbytery took up the case; and though certainly they, as a body, did but scanty justice to Mr. Burns and his work, they went boldly into the evidence on both sides. *Anonymous hearsay testimony was at an end.* Witnesses were summoned; ministers, elders, newspaper editors, all came forward and manfully gave their evidence in the presence of the public. Every statement was sifted, and every witness cross-questioned. No unproved charge was tolerated. No hearsay evidence was admitted. It was bold, open, honest, face-to-face examination throughout. The result was a large body of evidence, important and interesting, which was immediately published, so that every one might form his own judgment upon explicit testimony for and against. Mr. Burns, as the chief instrument, was summoned, and answered calmly for himself, both by letter and by oral statement. He was cross-questioned at great length, and was publicly called to admit, or deny, or explain various proceedings and expressions which the newspapers had reported, or which common rumour had circulated. In this way very important facts were elicited, bearing not simply upon the *general* truth or falsehood of the work, but upon this question, which is too much overlooked in such a case,—May not a revival work be substantially a work of God, and yet a considerable part of it pronounced unsatisfactory? That one-half of such a work comes to nought is no proof that the other may not stand; nay, that three-fourths of the work are doubtful does not demonstrate the hollowness of the rest. Let us take the good, and 'cast the bad away;' let us be thankful for the wheat, though growing alongside of tares, and not persist in holding up the *tares* as a specimen of the *wheat*.

In Dr. Kennedy's pamphlet, from the title to the last leaf, no name occurs save his own. Its pages contain a *resumé* of serious indictments against men *who are not named*, on the authority of witnesses *who are not named*. His censures, very broadly made, implicate some two or three hundred brethren in the different Churches throughout Scotland. His accusations, if true, ought to drive these ministers from their pulpits, as preachers of insidious error in the teeth of their own subscriptions. Yet not one of these brethren is named; no proof is led of these imputations. These brethren are condemned without the possibility of being able to answer the aspersions of their prosecutor. *

The Aberdeen examination, though conducted mostly by 'Moderates,' was fairly carried out. The Presbytery acted on the principle to which the apostle appealed,—'To whom I answered, It is not the manner of the Romans to deliver any man to die, *before he who is accused have the accusers face to face, and have licence to answer for himself concerning the crime laid against him*' (Acts 25:16). Dr. Kennedy has forgotten this. He has flung his reproaches broadcast over the Churches; he will not name the guilty 'hyper-evangelists,' nor will he tell us who gave him the information. If he is desirous to convince his deluded brethren of their error, he ought to name them; if he wishes to undeceive the public, he ought to produce witnesses.

Yet he speaks of himself thus: 'SAD, YEA, STRAINED TO BREAKING, must be the heart of one who seeks the glory of God and the salvation of souls, if he cannot share in the prevalent hopefulness and joy. Being one of those to whom the present movement has hitherto yielded more grief than gladness, I feel constrained to tell why I am A MOURNER AND APART' * (p. 13). I indicate the words that have struck me most, in this

---

* It must be kept in mind that the pamphlet not merely censures the work, but the men engaged in it; accusing them, without proof, of holding false doctrines, and of unscriptural proceedings, and of being under the influence of Satan as an angel of light. The objections against the work did require to be sustained by evidence; much more the charges against the brethren conducting it.

* But surely the writer of the pamphlet is not the only one who seeks the glory of God and the salvation of souls, as this would imply. He has *not* mourned 'apart,'

passage, by capitals, and I make no comment. 'A heart strained to breaking' would do justice to brethren, and would be willing to *prove* assertions against men who have also hearts that can at least be 'sad,' if not 'strained to breaking,' at the anonymous accusations published against them by one who has not, even in private, met them as a brother, to warn them of their errors.

The pamphlet may be divided into two parts,—the Facts, and the Conclusions from these. The former are few in number; the latter constitute the body of the work.

The 'facts' are not certified by any one: so we might set them aside. Some of them we can recognise, sadly coloured, or rather discoloured. Some we know to be unfounded. But even admitting them all, we aver that the conclusions are not justified. In past revivals, even in Ross-shire, things have been said and done quite as much fitted to create suspicion as anything that has occurred during the recent movement. Suppose I accept the facts, repulsive as some of them look, I do not see how they warrant the conclusion that the work cannot be divine. Offences will come; but is the gospel of none effect because of them? Can the Holy Spirit not work by poor and defective instruments? He wrought not only by the Calvinistic Whitefield, but the Arminian Wesley. We are not, surely, reckoned to be farther gone in 'error,' or more peculiar in practice, or more unguarded in statement, than the preachers of Methodism. Yet they are acknowledged as men who wrought a good work for England, in spite of blemishes. Will our opposing brethren only do us the justice which has been manifested towards the Wesleyans, and measure our work by the same standard as they measure theirs, making allowances for some things, it may be, which they dislike?

But the bulk of the pamphlet consists of inferences. Dr. Kennedy has *generalised* to an alarming extent. His facts are as a few grains of sand; his generalisations are mountains. Indeed, we suspect that he is conscious that his few facts will not bear out the multitude of his conclusions, for he does not try, in many cases, to connect the one with the other. He has *preconceived* the whole character of a Lowland revival and his remarks are founded upon this great *preconception*. In developing these preconceptions or theories, he makes use of both tele-

---

but has come forward to accuse his brethren of I know not how many evil things; things of which it would have been well to speak to them first in private, before making this public charge. The pamphlet is not what we should have expected from one 'mourning apart.'

scope and microscope,—the former to see afar off what other eyes cannot see; the latter to magnify all little things, so as to enable him to found very large conclusions upon them.

Unmingled condemnation of the movement pervades the pamphlet. No word of hope is spoken. No intimation of anything like joy at the announcement of a work like this, attested by so many brethren, or at the mere *possibility* of its being true! We call to mind here the words, 'Then tidings of these things came unto the ears of the church which was in Jerusalem; and they sent forth Barnabas, who, when he came, and had seen the grace of God, WAS GLAD; for he was a good man, and full of the Holy Ghost and of faith' (Acts 11:22). Did these early Christians judge the work *prematurely*? They certainly judged it *quickly*. What a contrast to what we find in the present pamphlet, where there is little else than the coldness of incredulity,—suspecting motives, and putting the worst construction on all that is done!

We have something to say for ourselves. We are not infallible. We cannot discern spirits. We are liable to misjudge. But we consider ourselves honest Christian men, who have no personal nor sinister object in view to bias our testimony. We have no preconceived views as to the likelihood or unlikelihood of such things being effected by such instruments. We consider ourselves competent witnesses, and we offer ourselves to the Church as such. We do not speak darkly; we do not bring indiscriminate imputations against brethren. We do not state facts without telling the source of our information; we do not pronounce opinions without furnishing the data on which our judgment is based. We feel that, without assumption of superiority, we may present ourselves to the Churches of the land, and say: Here are we, some hundreds of the servants of the Lord Jesus Christ. We testify of a great work that has been wrought amongst us; we give you every part of our evidence at first-hand, not at second-hand; we are men who have been,—some of us at least,—long in the ministry, till our eyes have grown dim with service; we know something of the nature of such a work; we have carefully watched and examined the present movement. Question us; we are ready to answer; we can give you reasons for what we believe and bear witness to. Will you receive charges against us, uncorroborated by evidence, and which we as honourable men declare to be untrue?

Are we, or are we not, credible and competent witnesses? Is there not one wise man amongst us? Is there no one of those who have taken part in the work whose testimony may be trusted, and whose opinion is worth listening to? In the great question of spiritual work, are

Lowland ministers not entitled to be heard? May one Northern brother, who has taken no part in the work, set them all aside, and give
sentence against them and against the work in which they have been
engaged, without obtaining from one of them the information which
they only could give? Surely the friends of the work are as fully entitled to be heard as its enemies!

Is Dr. Kennedy a minister of Christ? So are we. Does he work the
work of God? So do we. Does he preach the cross? So do we. Does
he labour for a harvest? So do we. Does he watch for souls as they
that must give account? So do we. Is he of the seed of the godly? So
are we. Is he jealous of the Master's honour and Jehovah's rights? So
are we. Is he careful to maintain purity of doctrine and holiness of
life? So are we. Is he, in the sight of God, thoroughly convinced of the
truth of what he says? So are we no less thoroughly convinced of the
certainty of that which we declare before God and man.

Our credibility and competency as witnesses in this matter may be
denied; but it must be *disproved* as well as *denied;* and the refusal to
admit our testimony by any one brother, however gifted, would argue
such self-confidence as to make us unwilling to entertain the suppo-
sition that the present writer would reject such testimony or distrust
such witnesses without adducing fully his reasons for doing so. Yet
the pamphlet before us assumes that no credit is to be attached to the
numerous statements of the men connected with the work, who offer
themselves as witnesses, but only to those of some unknown and un-
named brethren who have brought up an evil report against it.

I am not altogether surprised to find Dr. Kennedy condemning the
present religious movement in Scotland. He has not seen his way to
believe in any of those former Southern awakenings by which most
Scottish Christians have been gladdened. I do not judge him for this,
nor shall I the less call him an honoured servant of the Lord. His
Northern experiences seem to unfit him for appreciating the religion
of 'the Southron,' * as he designates us of the Lowlands. To his own
Master he stands or falls.

Of the awakenings at Kilsyth, Dundee, Perth, Aberdeen, under Mr.
Burns, Mr. M'Cheyne, Mr. Milne, and others, during the memorable
years preceding the Disruption, he thus writes in his interesting sketch
of his father's ministry:—

'The religious awakening which, a short time before his death,

---

* *The Days of the Fathers in Ross-shire,* pp. 119, 153, 240.

spread over various districts of Scotland, he did not regard with much hopefulness and pleasure. He expected but little permanent fruit as its result, and was much pained by the countenance given, in the excitement of that time, to manifest delusions. The experience of all his life tended to make him distrustful as to all awakening accompanied with violent bodily excitement, and he never failed to repress any such exhibitions whenever they appeared in his presence. His anticipations were, alas! too fully realised. The rich flush of blossom that then appeared withered prematurely and almost entirely away, and bitter disappointment awaited those who formed a more sanguine estimate than his of the fruit that might in the end be produced.'

Let those who passed through that earnest time say whether this strong censure is just or not; and let those who are to this day reaping the fruit of these awakenings judge whether the 'rich flush of blossoms' did thus wither away. My own remembrance of Kilsyth and Dundee is very different from Dr. Kennedy's; and my testimony to the results of that period would not be one of faded blossoms, but of much fruit to the glory of God.

I do not blame Dr. Kennedy for setting aside such testimonies as those of Mr. Burns, Mr. M'Cheyne, Mr. Gray (of Perth), Mr. Milne (of Perth), and many other such of the best men of that day. He is fully entitled, I admit, to form his own judgment on so momentous a matter; but then the fact of his judgment being so continuously against all those revival movements of other days, though attested by the wisest and godliest of the time, leads us to lay less stress upon that judgment when we find it opposed to us now.

I do not deny that there were many who did fall off in these days, after having promised well. But if any awakening, either in the North or South, were free from 'wayside' or 'stony-ground' or 'thorny-ground' hearers, I should say it was such an awakening as the Master had not led us to expect, and such as has not yet been witnessed on earth. To test the genuineness of a revival by these three kinds of hearers, and to make the existence of these a proof of its unreality, seems to me to be denying the meaning of that parable, and refusing the warning for which it was given. Wherever the true seed is sown, there will be found these three classes of false hearers, and these three kinds of unskilful or imperfect sowing. *

---

* In opposition to Dr. Kennedy's opinion I should like to quote two passages.

I have another reason for not being surprised at Dr. Kennedy's objections to the Southern revival. I find that many of the Ross-shire fathers who were the leaders in the Northern movement were men who had what is called the 'second-sight,' and who had the gift of prophecy. In pointing out this, I am not seeking to disparage these excellent men, nor to censure a brother for accepting their second-sight as a reality and the predictions as genuine. I am not desirous of raising any questions as to these things. Some may think that the evidence of the gifts of these noble men is sufficient, and I am not prepared to say that it is not so. They may have had the second-sight,

---

The first is Mr. M'Cheyne's opinion of the work of that period:—'It is my decided and solemn conviction in the sight of God, that a very remarkable and glorious work of God, in the conversion of sinners and edifying of saints, has taken place in this parish and neighbourhood. This work I have observed going on from the very beginning of my ministry in this place in November 1836, and it is continued to the present time; but it was much more remarkable in the autumn of 1839, when I was abroad on a mission of inquiry to the Jews, and when my place was occupied by the Rev. W.C. Burns. Previous to my going abroad, and for several months afterwards, the means used were of the ordinary kind. In addition to the services of the Sabbath, in the summer of 1837, a meeting was opened in the church on Thursday evenings for prayer, exposition of Scripture, reading accounts of missions, revivals of religion, etc. Sabbath schools were formed, private prayer meetings were encouraged, and two weekly classes for young men and young women were instituted with a very large attendance. These means were accompanied with an evident blessing from on high in many instances. But there was no visible or general movement among the people until August 1839, when, immediately after the beginning of the Lord's work at Kilsyth, the word of God came with such power to the hearts and consciences of the people here, and their thirst for hearing it became so intense, that the evening classes in the school-room were changed into densely crowded congregations in the church, and for nearly four months it was found desirable to have public worship almost every night. At this time, also, many prayer meetings were formed, some of which were strictly private or fellowship meetings, and others, conducted by persons of some Christian experience, were open to persons under concern about their souls. At the time of my return from the mission to the Jews, I found thirty-nine such meetings held weekly in connection with the congregation, and five of these were conducted and attended entirely by little children. At present, although many changes have taken place, I believe the number of these meetings is not much diminished' (pp. 66, 67). The second is Mr. Milne's:—'I had abundant opportunity of becoming intimately acquainted with Mr. Burns, as he lived and laboured with me constantly for between three and four months. I never knew any one who so fully and unfalteringly obeyed the apostolic precept, "Meditate upon these things, give thyself *wholly* to them." I was struck with his close walk with God, his much and earnest prayer,

and the instances recorded may be authentic. But then the men who possessed such prophetic gifts could not be expected to sympathise in a work where none of these were exhibited and claimed; and the biographer of these men will naturally look suspiciously upon the men of the South, who have not the peculiarities of the North, and question the depth of any movement going on under them. Let me give a few instances of what I refer to from Dr. Kennedy's book, *The Days of the Fathers:*—

'On another occasion he was bearing testimony against dis-

---

his habitual seriousness, the solemnising effect which his presence seemed to have wherever he went, and his almost unwearied success in leading those with whom he conversed to anxious, practical, heart-searching concern about their state in God's sight. In public, his ministrations were chiefly of an awakening nature, addressed to the unconverted. With this view, his subjects were always wisely selected, being such as included fundamental points,—man's lost state as a sinner; its marks and consequences; man's helplessness as a sinner; the vanity of all his endeavours to justify or sanctify himself, and the certain and everlasting ruin of all who should persevere in such attempts; Christ Jesus, His righteousness, its alone sufficiency, its *perfect* freeness, its *immediate* gift to all who believe; the blessed effects of such faith; the Holy Spirit, His work in convincing and converting, and the danger of resisting Him. These subjects were treated more subjectively than objectively, which Mr. Burns was the better enabled to do from having much intercourse with people under concern, who had fully opened up their minds to him. The effect of his preaching was also aided by the unusual earnestness and solemnity of his delivery, as well as by the densely crowded state of the church, and the spirit of prayer and expectation in which very many came to the meetings. In compliance with the language of the query, I have spoken of the chief human instrument; but I am persuaded, both from what I saw and felt at the time, and from what I have since known of the permanent and blessed results, that a greater than man was among us: "Not by power, nor by might, but by my Spirit." I never witnessed before, nor have I since, such manifest tokens of God's gracious presence as were vouchsafed us during several of the first months of last year. I can only say, in the words of Jonathan Edwards, "The goings of God were then seen in His sanctuary, God's day was a delight, and His tabernacles were amiable. Our public assemblies were then beautiful; the congregation was alive in God's service, every one earnestly intent on the public worship, every hearer eager to drink in the words of the minister as they came from his mouth." What he also mentions of the much weeping and deep concern manifested under the preaching of the word is also true in regard to the meetings here, but is noticed in a subsequent query' (pp. 58, 59). It is the work thus attested that Dr. Kennedy speaks of as giving countenance to 'manifest delusions,' and which was regarded 'without much hopefulness and pleasure.'

honest dealing, assuring his hearers that, sooner or later, the Lord would punish all who held the balances of deceit. As an example of how the Lord sometimes, even in this life, gives proof of His marking the sin of dishonesty, he repeated an anecdote which was current at the time. A woman who had been engaged in selling milk, with which she always mingled a third of water, and who had made some money by her traffic, was going with her gains to America. During the voyage she kept her treasure in a bag, which was always under her pillow. There was a monkey on board the ship that was allowed to go at large, and that in course of its wanderings came to the milkwoman's hammock, in rummaging which it found the bag of gold. Carrying it off, the monkey mounted the rigging, and, seating itself aloft on a spar, opened the bag and began to pick out the coins. The first it threw out into the sea, and the second and third it dropped on the deck, and so on, till a third of all the contents of the bag had sunk in the ocean, the owner of the bag being allowed to gather off the deck just what she had fairly earned by her milk. One of Mr. Lachlan's hearers remembered, while listening to this anecdote, that he had in his trunk at home a bundle of banknotes, which he had got by the sale of diluted whisky. Feeling very uneasy, he hurried to his house after the sermon was over. It was dark before he arrived, and, kindling a pine torch, he hastened to the place where he kept his money, afraid that it had been taken away. Holding the torch with one hand, while he turned over the notes with the other, a flaming ember fell right down into the midst of the treasure, and before the man, bewildered as he was, could rescue them, as many of the notes were consumed as exactly represented the extent to which he had diluted the whisky.'—pp. 64, 65.

'Once, while preaching there on a Sabbath, he said, in a very marked and emphatic way, "There is one now present, who, before coming into the meeting, was engaged in bargaining about his cattle, regardless alike of the day and of the eye of the Lord. Thou knowest that I speak the truth; and listen while I declare to thee, that if the Lord ever hath mercy on thy soul, thou wilt yet be reduced to seek, as alms, thy daily bread." The confidence with which this was said was soon and sorely tried, and he passed a sleepless night, under the fear that he had spoken unadvisedly. At breakfast next morning, in his father's house, several neighbouring farmers were present, one of whom said to him as they sat at table, "How did you know that I was selling my heifers yesterday to the drover?" "Did you do so?" my father quietly asked him. "I can't deny it," was the farmer's answer. Directing on him one of his searching glances, the minister said, "Remember the warning that was given you, for you will lose either your soul or your substance." "But will you not tell me how you knew it?" the farmer asked. The only reply to this was, in the words of Scripture, "The secret of the Lord is with them that fear Him." '—p. 199.

'On another occasion, in the same place, while warning sinners of their danger in a Christless state, he suddenly paused, and in a subdued and solemn tone said, "There is a sinner in this place, very ripe for destruction, who shall this night be suddenly summoned to a judgment-seat." Next morning the neighbours observed flames issuing from a hut not far from the "meeting-house," which was occupied by a woman notorious for immorality, and in which, when they were able to enter, they found but the charred bones of its miserable tenant.'—pp. 199, 200.

'It was quite extraordinary how her mind would be led to take an interest in the cause of Christ in places and in countries of which she knew not even the names. Instances of this might be given so remarkable, that I cannot venture to risk my credibility by recording them. One only will be given. Coming to me once, with an anxious expression on her face, she asked if there was any minister in a certain district, which she could only indicate by telling that it was not far from a place of which she knew the name. I told her there was. "But why do you wish to know?" I asked. "I saw him lately," was her answer, "fixing a wing to each of his sides, and rising on these wings into the air till he was very high, and then suddenly he fell, and was dashed to pieces on the ground;" and she added, "I think if there is such a minister, that he has but a borrowed godliness, and that his end is near." There was just such a minister, and his end was near, for before a week had passed I received the tidings of his death.'—p. 224.

'Having attended at Contin on a Communion Sabbath, when

my father officiated, after all the other communicants had taken their places at the table, he, for some reason which he did not live to reveal, still remained in his seat. The minister said, "There is still some communicant here who has not come forward, and till that person takes a seat at the table I cannot proceed with the service." Another verse was then sung, but "the merchant from Kiltarlity" did not come. He was not in the minister's eye, though there was some one on his spirit, when he said, "I implore you to come forward, for this is your last opportunity of showing forth the Lord's death till He come; for, if I am not greatly mistaken, you will not reach your home in life after the close of this service." The merchant then came forward, and no sooner had he taken his seat at the table than the minister said, "We may now proceed with the service." On the dismissal of the congregation on Monday, the merchant set his face on his home, but while crossing the ford of the Conon, he was carried down by the stream and was drowned.'—pp. 234, 235.

'Mr. Fraser's sudden death, which occurred a few years before his own, deeply affected my father. The tidings reached Killearnan after he had gone out to church, on the day of the monthly lecture. To the surprise of all, he expressed, in public prayer that day, his persuasion that a breach had been made on the walls of Zion in the North by the removal of one of the eminent servants of the Lord. On coming out of church, and being informed of Mr. Fraser's death, he said, "I was prepared for this." '—p. 244.

'His anticipations of the result of the conflict were very alarming, and to some seemed prophetic. Often did he distinctly announce the event of the Disruption. Dr. Macdonald has told me with what surprise he heard him once say, while preaching in the church of Ferintosh in 1829, "This crowded church shall yet become a place into which none who fear the Lord will dare to enter;" adding, "Not long before this change takes place I shall be removed to my rest, but many who now hear me shall see it." '—p. 253.

'His last pastoral visit was to a pious couple in the east end of his parish, who were apparently dying, and very anxious to see him. The husband was one of his elders, but both in intellect and in spirituality excelled by his wife. Among other questions, he asked them individually, "Do you believe that your affliction was appointed by God in the everlasting covenant?" The wife was first addressed, and her reply was, "I believe that it is permitted by God in His providence, but I have not attained to believe that it was ordered in the covenant." The husband's answer was, "I cannot even say what my wife has just said." "You are a step behind her, Donald," his minister said; "and as surely as she is before you in this, she will be before you in heaven." And so it happened, though the husband was both older and a greater invalid than his wife.'—pp. 255, 256.

I admit that we are not able to produce any such instances of prophetic discernment in the South; and if a Southern movement is to be thus tested, it must be set aside. But it may be a genuine work of God for all that. One nurtured amid the peculiarities of the North, and taught to look on these gifted men of Ross-shire as the true types of Christian ministers, on their sermons as the true models of preaching, and on their work as the true work of the Spirit of God, may be led to suspect other men, other preaching, and other work; but then we may suspect him in his judgment of us. His bias is against us. The absence of certain characteristics in the South must be an important element in his estimate of us; and we are inclined to ask, How far can we accept the judgment of one whose prepossessions in favour of the supernatural are such as to repel him from a work where these characteristics do not exist? I am not questioning the reality of the Ross-shire work, nor decrying the excellency of 'the Fathers.' I am merely pointing out a striking peculiarity, which inclines me to accept the opinion of a Northern as to a work in the South with considerable hesitation and abatement. His standard differs from ours. His point of view is not at all the same as ours. He claims certain things which we do not. He demurs to some things to which we do not.

I make the above remarks the more unhesitatingly, because of the author's strong statements in reference to those who question these supernatural gifts. Of the instances above given, he says 'they are indubitable facts' (p. 200); and that they are tokens of God's presence (with these ministers) 'to a simple and uneducated people, unable *to appreciate the standing evidences of the gospel*' (*ib.*). I am slow to believe that the gospel needs such *additional evidences in its favour* as these supernatural gifts furnish; nor can I think that the Highlanders are so 'uneducated' as the above statement would indicate. Before saying some of his strong things against Mr. Moody and his alleged un-scriptural teachings, Dr. Kennedy should have reconsidered such a statement. It is just such a sentence as an Irvingite might have written.

But Dr. Kennedy writes keen censure against those who stand in doubt of these stories:—

'The improbability of such things to the minds of some *is owing to their own utter estrangement from the Lord.* This is not the only secret connected with a life of godliness which is hidden from them. They know not yet some secrets in that life of which it is death to be ignorant. It is not to its occasional accessories merely that they are strangers, but to its very essentials; and yet who so ready as they to pass judgment on every one of its mysteries? It is a strange fact, that the only subject of which one can know absolutely nothing without special teaching from on high is, of all others, the one on which the most benighted of all "the children of darkness" thinks himself qualified to pronounce.'

All this is very startling. The condemnation thus pronounced on those who, as he writes, 'shake their wise heads' over these stories, and over the imprudence of their narrator, is certainly too harsh. I regret much, not that Dr. Kennedy has told these stories, but that he has so committed himself to them, and so unadvisedly censured those who, without in the least 'sneering' at them, feel constrained to ask for fuller evidence.

In many 'Southrons' these peculiar stories will engender suspicion of the whole of Ross-shire. In my own mind they do not. I believe in the work wrought in the North by those pious men whose doings Dr. Kennedy records. I have long delighted in gathering up every stray fragment of their blessed history. I can separate what is doubtful from what is certain, what is unscriptural from what is not. They were men of whom the world was not worthy, and they shall be in everlasting remembrance. Their names have long been familiar to me, though I have thought that the way in which they were sometimes eulogised by biographers, and compared or rather contrasted with others, indicated too much of the supercilious and the censorious.

The existence of these gifts cannot be regarded as any proof of the greater *depth* of the Northern work. They may be appealed to as such. I cannot accept the appeal. I remember what the apostle wrote: 'Though

I speak with the tongues of men and of angels, *and have not charity,* I am become as sounding brass, or a tinkling cymbal. And though I have the gift of prophecy, and understand all mysteries, and all knowledge; and though I have all faith, so that I could remove mountains, *and have not charity,* I am nothing' (1 Cor. 13:1,2). I am no scoffer at the men or their sayings. I shall gladly accept evidence of their gifts. But I object to the strong condemnation pronounced by Dr. Kennedy on those who stand in doubt. It makes the heart 'sad'—I will not say 'strained to breaking.'

To one who has observed how the credulous and the incredulous are often exhibited in the same minds; how those who believe too much in one direction believe too little in another, it will not seem strange that there should be, among some, the disposition to question the genuineness of the late awakening. Nor would I judge those who stand aloof. Yet this I would say, that it would be wiser and nobler not to be on the watch for declensions, not to predict failures, not to glean and retail unfavourable stories or odd sayings. Offences will come, as the Master has forewarned us. The love of many will wax cold. Ephesus will leave her first love. But what of these things? Are they strange things in the history of the Church? Have they not been from the beginning? May not the work be true after all? And is there any good work wrought by the servants of God of which evil things have not been said? Yes, and sometimes *truly* said. For do not the best amongst us sometimes do rash things, form foolish plans, go into sad indiscretions, and speak unadvisedly with our lips? 'If Thou, Lord, shouldest mark iniquity, who shall stand?' But our gracious Lord and Master judgeth us not as man judgeth. He knoweth our frame, and utters no harsh censures. He does not mock our poor work, which daily betrays the imperfection of the instrument. He speaks through stammering tongues, and does His mightiest things by bruised reeds. He does not come to us as the critic, or the judge, or the fault-finder, but speaks in gentleness: 'I have set before thee an open door, and no man can shut it, for thou hast little strength, yet hast kept my word, and hast not denied my name' (Rev. 3:8).

As the writer does not believe in the 'Southron' revivals, either former or recent, so it seems to me that he has no confidence in the piety or theology of the Lowlands; for the pamphlet is evidently not directed against Mr. Moody merely, but *against the brethren of all Churches who gathered round him.* It is the current theology that he aims at throughout. The American brother is not the main object of animadversion; and though no man is named, many are struck at. We were reminded of a verse in the book of Esther,—'He thought scorn to lay hands on Mordecai alone; wherefore he sought to destroy all the Jews that were throughout the whole kingdom, even the people of Mordecai' (Esther 3:6).

The pamphlet arraigns those connected with the present movement, and enumerates different points of doctrine on which they are unsound. They seem to be teachers of serious error, subverters of foundation-truth; the blind leading the blind, and both falling into the ditch.

Yet we honestly subscribe the Westminster Confession. We believe in Christ's redemption of His chosen Church; in the efficacy of His blood and the perfection of His righteousness. We believe in human impotence, in the bondage of the human will, in the enmity of the human heart to God. We believe in the sovereignty of Jehovah, and His eternal purpose. We believe in the absolute necessity of the Holy Spirit's work, alike before and after conversion. At the same time we preach a free and world-wide gospel; we proclaim a free and world-wide invitation to sinners; we present to every sinner a gracious welcome to Christ, without any preliminary qualification whatsoever. We bid no man wait till he has ascertained his own election, or can produce evidence of regeneration, or sufficient repentance, or deep conviction. We tell every man, *as he is,* to go to the Saviour this moment, assured that he will not be cast out or sent away. Whatever controversy there may be about the word 'assurance,' we hold that there can be none about 'peace with God,' and that we are bound to press upon every man this peace to which God is calling the sinner, and without which there can be no acceptable nor joyful service, seeing that all true religion begins with peace and reconciliation; for an unreconciled sinner cannot be a welcome worshipper. 'Peace with God,' as the *immediate* result of a believed gospel, is what the apostles preached. 'Peace with God,' not as the result of a certain amount of experience or feeling, but as flowing directly from the light of the cross, is that which we are commanded to preach as the glad tidings of great joy to the sinner.

No sentence is quoted from any of the accused. They are not allowed to speak for themselves. Their creed is written for them by another, and sentiments are ascribed to them which they do not hold. They are said to deny or ignore certain great truths, which they neither deny nor ignore. It would have been juster to give their errors *in their own words.* This would have prevented the imputation of one-sidedness or unfairness, into which, often unintentionally, the best are betrayed in controversy. Those who have read the controversial works of John Henry Newman must have been struck with the singular fairness which he manifests towards his opponents. He either quotes them *in extenso*, that they may do themselves justice, or else he states their arguments so fully, so strongly, that he seems to be reasoning against himself. More than once we have wondered at the pains he takes to put an opponent's position in the strongest way he can. Some of his statements on justification by faith are not only clear, but beautiful; not the less so because they were made by him in order to be overthrown.

In the present pamphlet we have nothing of that nobility of spirit, that is quite as anxious to do justice to an opponent as to the writer himself. *Full quotations* from the writings of the erring brethren would have gone far to prevent the complaint of misrepresentation which will inevitably be made in the present case.

I am not entitled to give my interpretation of another man's sentiments as equivalent to his own statements. He does not necessarily hold what I think he holds; and even if he cannot wholly question the accuracy of my construction, he may object most strongly to the colouring which I have given, and to the inferences which I have drawn. 'Paul, thou art permitted to speak for thyself,' ought to have been remembered in the present pamphlet. I am within the mark when I say, that during the last ten months there have been about a thousand speakers, and ten times that number of addresses and expositions. But not one of these thousand is appealed to, not one of these ten thousand is cited. Yet all these brethren are condemned by one who has only heard one or two of them, and these one or two perhaps but once, at most twice. The indiscriminate censure flung upon them, both as to doctrine and practice, may irritate, but cannot profit; may be resented, but cannot be listened to with patient teachableness, as coming from one who, in true humility, was willing to remind himself of his own liability to err while sitting in judgment on his erring brethren.

I do not mean to say that quotations from addresses, or even from published works, would have sufficed. Extracts are sometimes given in controversy, so limited and dislocated, that an opponent is made to say what he never intended to do. Scripture has been treated in this way, and so have uninspired men. When writing on one subject, an author confines himself to that; so that, if he had written nothing more, inferences might be drawn unfavourable to his soundness, especially by those in whose minds one idea so predominates as to destroy the proportions of all the rest. If I preach a course of sermons on Christ the Prophet, shall I be accused of denying Christ the Priest, because

I confine myself rigidly to the theme in hand? If, in a particular discourse or book, I dwell exclusively on the blood, shall I be charged with denying the righteousness of the Substitute? If I try to disentangle a perplexed sinner from the mazes in which he has involved himself by mixing up the work of the Spirit and the work of Christ, shall I be charged with denying the Spirit's work? If I preach on the words, 'Believe on the Lord Jesus Christ,' and restrict myself to the apostle's words just as he delivered them, must I be accused of denying the sovereignty of God or human impotence? If I preach a sermon or write a tract on the glad tidings emanating from the cross, and if I should happen, either through one-sidedness of nature, or momentary forgetfulness of all else, or the desire of presenting, vividly and alone, the glorious gospel to the sinner, to omit direct mention of the law, shall I be said to refuse the law its proper place; nay, to set it aside altogether? If I try to remove certain mystifications that have been cast over faith, must I be charged with holding it to be bare intellectual belief, when I have elsewhere stated that it connects itself not only with truth and with testimony, but with a promise and a person?

If, then, I am to convince or confute another, I must first accurately represent his views, lest I be merely pulling down what I myself had built up. And in representing his views, I must do so fully, not culling isolated sentences or peculiar expressions, but giving his statements accurately, in their completeness; not substituting my inferences for his opinions, and not giving the one-half of his teachings as if it were the whole. Fairness to the truth, justice to a brother, responsibility to God and to the Church, all demand this.

When Dr. Kennedy says, 'I heard the leading teacher repeatedly' (p. 17), I wish he had stated *where,* and *how often;* for some of us have heard him at least one hundred times, and we have not been able to discover in his teaching what Dr. Kennedy has done. My own reminiscences of Mr. Moody are widely different from Dr. Kennedy's. But I do not dwell on this; because the pamphlet is not really directed against the 'leading teacher,' but against the various ministers who associated themselves with him, or, as the writer affirms, 'sat as disciples at the feet of one whose teaching only showed his ignorance even of the principles of the doctrine of Christ' (pp. 15, 16).

It is, as I have said, the theology of the Lowlands that Dr. Kennedy has summoned to his tribunal, and against which he utters such hard impeachments. The reader is left in doubt whether the real gospel is preached in the South; or rather he is left in no doubt as to this,—that it is not preached at all. The 'Southron' has accepted 'another gospel,' which suits better his 'starched English' (*Days of the Fathers*, p. 42) than it does the free and stubborn tongue of the Gael.

I confess that I do not understand what 'hyper-evangelism' is. I know what 'hyper-Calvinism,' or even 'hyper-hyper-Calvinism' is; but I do not, even with the explanation in the pamphlet, comprehend what 'hyper-evangelism' can be. * I know what 'another gospel' means, because the apostle, who gave us the expression, has showed us, in the same epistle where it occurs, what it was in Galatia; and how it exhibited itself in putting restrictions on the freeness of the gospel, in mingling law with gospel, in destroying the simplicity of faith, in adding something to the finished work of Christ,—something to be done by the sinner himself, in addition to what Christ has done, to give the weary rest. This Galatian gospel raised a barrier between the sinner and the cross; it tried to intercept the flying manslayer in his way to the city of refuge; it made the way to Christ a long, dark, laborious, uncertain by-path; it set salvation afar off, and made the sinner's reception of it one of the most painful and complex of all processes, a thing of uncertainty to the last. I should not certainly like to preach 'another gospel;' but I should like to be very sure that what I preach is really 'another gospel' before I give it up. I should not like to be more evangelical than Paul; yet I should like to be as evangelical as he, preaching as free a gospel, and saying as broadly and unconditionally as he did at Antioch, in a sermon where *no mention of law* or of sovereignty is made, 'By Him all that believe are justified from all things.' And here I would notice, that in the Acts of the Apostles we have many specimens of apostolical preaching to promiscuous multitudes, yet in not one of them is the law introduced. The apostles con-

---

* 'Hyper-evangelism I call it, because of *the loud professions of evangelism* made by those who preach it, and because it is just an extreme application of some truths, to the neglect of others which are equally important parts of the great system of evangelic doctrine' (p. 16). Perhaps *some* have made these loud professions;' but it was hardly fair to bring such a charge against so many brethren, for I have not heard any such 'loud professions' from those with whom I have been associated. Perhaps there may be as 'loud professions' on the other side. I do not know; nor would thus accuse any man. At any rate, 'loud professions' cannot, with any correctness, be called 'hyper-evangelism;' and though 'extreme statements of truth' might be called either hyper-evangelical or anti-evangelical, they cannot admit of the name 'hyper-evangelistic.' This is a misnomer. If I preach more than the gospel warrants, or less than it warrants, I may be an *imperfect* evangelist, but I can hardly be called a hyper-evangelist.'

fined themselves to the glad tidings concerning Christ and His cross. Christ crucified was that which was preached for conviction and conversion. Peter did not say to his hearers, 'Ye have broken the ten commandments,' but, 'Ye have crucified Christ.' This was the sword which the apostles used for smiting the sinner's conscience; this was the hammer which they brought down with such awful force upon his head. I might charge some of our Northern men with ignoring the cross as the divine instrument for conviction much more truly than they could charge me with ignoring the law. I do not ignore the law; I know that 'the law is good if a man use it lawfully.' The question before us is, Do we use it lawfully? Do we give it the place which God has assigned to it? Do we preach it as the apostles did?

Let me now come to the charges against us in detail; and as many of these are contained in brief expressions scattered through the pamphlet, I first call attention to these. They are such as the following:—

'Men are sadly forgetful, and *madly bold*' (p. 13).

I do not deny our too frequent forgetfulness of the needful lesson referred to by the writer. I admit the necessity of caution, and the danger of rash or premature affirmations as to a work of God. But I cannot concede that we have been 'madly bold.' We are entitled to look at a professed change from darkness to light, and to judge of its genuineness. We ought to be careful as to such a judgment; but when evidence is presented, we cannot help forming a judgment, and this without being 'madly bold.' The notable thing about the conversions recorded in Scripture is, that the *profession of a change was accepted at once*, and he who professed was received at once as a believer (as in the case of Simon Magus), before there was time for the exhibition of evidence. That this was done by inspired apostles *is a valid reason for our doing the same.* That it was not their inspiration that guided their judgment, is evident from the fact of their being sometimes deceived. Their proceedings are undoubtedly recorded for our imitation. Had they been uninspired men, *some* amongst us would have refused to accept their example, as being that of fallible men; yet *these* will not allow us now to imitate them, because they were inspired, and therefore infallible!

'There is some reason to fear that his (Satan's) hand is *on the agents as well* as the subjects of the work, when neither are careful to apply the test of truth' (p. 14).

I wish the writer had given proof of *Satanic influence operating on us the agents, and on others the subjects*, of the work. It is a serious thing for one brother to come up to another and say, You are under Satanic influence. What would Dr. Kennedy answer if I were saying this to him? We *are* 'careful to apply the test of truth,' and to test ourselves as well as others with jealous scrutiny.

'Many seem to think, that *if they choose* to call a religious movement a work of grace, no fault should be found with any instrumentality employed in producing it' (p. 15).

Of course this language implies that we quite disregard any scriptural rule or guidance. 'We *choose* to call it a work of grace!' We employ any kind of instrumentality! No; we have not acted in any such way, and the accusation thus keenly pointed we warmly deny.

'A call to repentance *never issues from their trumpet*. In their view there is no place for repentance, either before or after conversion' (p. 18).

This is quite at variance with fact. I wish that *proof had been given* of such a statement, or some credible and competent witness, who had attended *all* the meetings, and heard *all* the addresses, had been called; otherwise, how can any one receive the sweeping invective, 'A call to repentance NEVER issues from their trumpet'? I myself have heard many such calls to repentance issuing from their trumpet. The above statement could be easily disproved. As a Christian brother, I ask Dr. Kennedy for his evidence. I am ready to give mine to the contrary. Produce your witnesses. The cause in court is a very sacred one; anonymous rumour will not suffice.

It is unfair to blame Mr. Moody for casual expressions on regeneration, and repentance, and faith—and to charge him with holding that man can work these changes in himself, without the Holy Spirit. Mr. Moody does not hold this; and they who seize hold of some stray words of his which *seem* to intimate this, should remember that Calvin, in his well-known *Institutes,* has given us what *they* must regard as a much more offensive and unsound announcement. The third chapter of his third book is entitled, *'Regeneration by Faith;'* and the first section of this chapter is to show how 'repentance follows faith, and is produced by it;' and to expose 'the error of those who take a contrary view.' He then proceeds: 'That repentance not only always follows faith, but is produced by it, ought to be without controversy. Those who think that repentance precedes faith, instead of flowing from or being produced by it, as the fruit by the tree, *have never understood its nature,* and are moved to adopt that view on very insufficient grounds....There is no semblance of reason in the absurd procedure of those who, that they may begin with repentance, prescribe to their neophytes certain days during which they are to exercise themselves in repentance, and *after these are elapsed* admit them to communion in gospel grace. I allude to great numbers of Anabaptists, those of them especially who plume themselves on being spiritual. What then? Can true repentance exist without faith? By no means; under the term repentance is comprehended the whole work of turning to God, of which not the least important part is faith. The term repentance is derived in the Hebrew from conversion, or turning again, and in the Greek, from a change of mind and purpose; nor is the thing meant inappropriate to both derivations, for it is substantially this, that withdrawing from ourselves, we turn to God, and laying aside the old, put on a new mind' (*Institutes,* b. iii., ch. 13).

It is impossible here to take up the question of repentance, and its connection with faith. It is evident, however, that the repentance which does not come *from believing* must be simply that of the natural conscience. It was the preaching of a crucified Christ at Pentecost that produced repentance. It is not said, 'They shall mourn, and look to Him whom they have pierced;' but, 'They shall look to Him whom they have pierced, and mourn.' Our old and best divines were very strong and full upon this point, accounting the opposite to be the Popish doctrine of a man's being able to recommend himself to God, and prepare himself for Christ, by mortifications and penances. Let us read a few of these precious teachings of the olden time. Thus wrote old John Davidson in his Catechism: 'When I sall aske you, what is craved of us *after that* we are joined to Christ by faith, and made truly righteous in Him, ye sall answere, We must repent and become new persons.' James Melvil in his Old Catechism says: 'What is thy repentance? The *effect of this faith,* with a sorrow for my sins by-past, and purpose to amend in time to come.' I need not add others. (See the *Marrow of Modern Divinity,* with Thomas Boston's Notes.) *

---

* 'It is not sound doctrine,' says Dr. Colquhoun, 'to teach that Christ will receive none but the true penitent, or that none else is warranted to come by faith to Him for salvation. The evil of that doctrine is, that it sets needy sinners on spinning repentance, as it were, out of their own bowels, and on bringing it with

In a letter from Mr. Moody lying before me I read the following tence: 'I believe that no man can come unto Jesus except the Fa draw him;' and he goes on to say that the power to believe must c from above. He complains also that expressions have been separated from their connection with the whole statement, and that in their isolation they appear quite different in meaning from what they were intended by the speaker. The following extract from Dr. Kennedy will show this:—

> 'Hundreds of ministers have I seen sitting as disciples at the feet of one whose teaching only showed his ignorance even of "the principles of the doctrine of Christ;" who, to their face, called the Churches which they represented 'first-class mobs;' was organising before their eyes an association, for religious objects, outside the Churches, which may yet prove as troublesome as the naked forces of the world; was casting ridicule on their old forms of worship, which they were sworn to uphold; and was proposing to convert prayer meetings into occasions of religious amusement, a change which he certainly did not ask them to approve without giving them a specimen, which excited the laughter of thousands, and gave to themselves a sensation of merrymaking in the house of the Lord' (pp. 15, 16).

On this extraordinary passage I may remark, that Mr. Moody did *not* call *the Churches* 'first-class mobs.' He spoke of the great multitudes before him as needing organisation in order to do effective work, and said that, unless they were properly organised, they were only 'mobs' or 'crowds';—'first class,' indeed, but still as useless as 'mobs' for any efficient service. Was this ill-spoken? The expression 'mob' might be a strong one, but the meaning was so obvious, and the thing so true, that only dislocation from the proper connection could have perverted the words into a cause of offence. What Mr. Moody urged was, system and organisation; what he deplored was, confusion and disorder among Christian workers. His plans may or may not have been approved of, but the necessity for some plan or system is sufficiently ob-

---

them to Christ, instead of coming to Him by faith to receive it from Him. If none be invited but the true penitent, then impenitent sinners are *not bound* to come to Christ, and cannot be blamed for not coming' (*View of Evangelical Repentance,* pp. 27, 28). And again he remarks: 'Saving faith is *the mean* of true repentance; and this repentance is not the mean but *the end* of that faith' (*Ib.* p. 164).

vious. Who of us does not feel the desirableness of organising our members, and laying out their districts and their work? The concluding part of the statement,—as to turning prayer meetings into 'occasions of religious amusement,'—is such a perversion of all that Mr. Moody ever stated or desired, that no one who heard him even occasionally, and knew his thorough earnestness, will credit the statement. There are hundreds of ministers and elders who will give evidence that it is wholly without foundation. If Dr. Kennedy would give *the whole* of Mr. Moody's statement, and not a mere fragment of it, the reader would be able to judge of its accuracy, and to see how entirely the obnoxious expression owed its objectionable character to its fragmentary state. There is an amount of unfairness and one-sidedness about these representations such as shakes our confidence in the accuracy of the whole pamphlet. In religious controversy we ought above all things to study *fairness and justice;* never to seek to catch an opponent tripping; never to try to make him say what he did not intend; and never to rest an appeal to the public on the critic's own interpretations of his opponent's argument, when the *ipsissima verba* from his own lips or pen can be produced.

'By a free gospel they can only intend to indicate a gospel that suits a sinner's disposition' (p. 19).

By a free gospel we are said to mean 'a gospel that suits a sinner's disposition;' nay, we 'can *only* intend' to indicate this!—But indeed we do not mean any such blasphemy as is imputed to us. We just mean the free gospel of the grace of God, which certainly does not suit the sinner's *dispositions,* though it admirably suits his *case.* Our *intentions* are not to *destroy* the gospel, but to *magnify* it. It is not seemly to impute such evil intentions. What if we were making such imputations against the author? Hard things have often been spoken against the 'Highland gospel.' I would not repeat them.

'The favourite doctrine of sudden conversion is practically a complete evasion of the necessity of repentance' (p. 19).

As for sudden conversions, we admit that we believe in them; inasmuch as all the conversions recorded in Scripture were sudden; nor do we remember any one that was not so. We but follow in the footsteps of apostles; all the more because we know they were inspired, and could not err. They have uttered no warning to us against sudden conversions. They have not said to us, You are not entitled to act as we do in regard to these; for we are infallible, you are fallible. They so speak and act as to lead us to follow their steps. In truth, *all conversions must be sudden if they are the work of the Holy Ghost.* They who deny such suddenness must believe the process of conversion to be in part a human one.

I have been much struck with some interesting cases of conversion recorded by Dr. Kennedy in his *Days of the Fathers.* They seem to have been *sudden,* and not to have been preceded by repentance or conviction of sin at all. They are as follow:—

'If there was one on earth that seemed quite beyond the reach of grace, it was old "Colin of the peats." Able yet to walk, he was regularly in church. After a Sabbath on which he was observed to have a wakeful, earnest expression on his deeply furrowed face, he came to his minister. "I saw a most beautiful one last Sabbath," the old man said as he sat down in the study. "Where did you see him?" he was asked. "In the sermon," was Colin's answer. "What was his appearance, Colin" "Oh, he was fairer than the sons of men; I can't tell what he was like, for he was altogether lovely." His minister then asked, "What effect had the sight of him on your heart?" " Oh, he quite took my heart from me," was Colin's simple and touching answer. This was all that he, then in his dotage, could tell about the change through which he passed' (p. 214).

'On a Saturday, as she sat by the fire in her bothy in Lochbroom, the idea of going to Killearnan came into her mind. Whence or how it came to her she could not tell, but she found it in her mind, and she could not shake it out. She rose from her seat, threw on her cloak, and started for Killearnan. She had never been there before, although she had often heard it spoken of. The journey was long and lonesome, but she kept on her way; and asking direction as she went on, she at last reached the old church of Killearnan as the people were assembling on the Sabbath morning. Following the people, she entered the church. During the sermon the voice of the Son of God was heard by Mary's quickened soul. She saw His beauty as no child of darkness ever saw it, and with her heart she said, before she left the church that day, "I am the Lord's" ' (pp. 219, 220).

'Among those who came from the West was one of whom those who knew her used to say that she was twice married in the same hour. During an excursion to the West my father preached in Strathbran, which, though now a waste wilderness almost throughout, then contained a considerable population. A marriage party arrived before the hour appointed for preaching, and having a considerable distance to travel to their home, were anxious to start immediately after the ceremony. The minister agreed to marry them at once. During his address, while commending the love of Christ, and presenting first of all His offer of marriage to each of the parties, the Lord applied the word with power to the heart of the bride, and before the marriage ceremony was over she gave herself to the Lord' (p. 235).

'Returning to Dingwall after the peace, he resided there till his death. Not long after his return, as he was dressing himself on a morning early in August, he was seized with an unaccountable desire to go to Cromarty. He had never been there before, and was conscious of no inducement to visit it, but he could not repress the feeling that had so suddenly seized him. He started on the journey, not knowing whither or wherefore he went. Reaching Cromarty before noon, he followed groups of people who were gathering to an eminence above the town. It was the Saturday of a communion season there. My father preached outside in Gaelic, and Hector was a hearer. The doctrine preached that day the Lord applied with power to his heart, and before the sermon was over he had given himself to the Lord' (pp. 237, 238).

Had these cases been recorded in the Lowlands, or in connection with the recent movement, what could the writer of *Hyper-Evangelism* have said? Sudden conversions! No convictions! No repentance! Only a supposed vision of Christ! All delusion! Had any of us ventured on the decided statement, 'that before the sermon was over he had given himself to the Lord,' or 'before the marriage ceremony was over she gave herself to the Lord,' what would have been said of our presumption? Would it not have been represented as 'a complete evasion of the necessity of repentance?'

Men, anxious to secure a certain result, and *determined to produce it,* do not like to think of a controlling will to whose sovereign behests they must submit, and of the necessity of almighty power being at work, whose action must be regulated by another will than theirs' (p. 21).

In the above sentence the charge brought against us is of a fearful kind. The words are unguarded and unadvised. Are we really what we are represented here to be? Are we such self-willed rebels, bent on our own plans, hating the sovereignty of God, and disliking the thought of any other will but our own; yet ministers of Christ? Impossible.

'This *selfish earnestness*, this *proud resolve* to make a *manageable business of conversion-work*, is intolerant of any recognition of the sovereignty of God' (p. 21).

I suppose we must just submit to the above reproach. Could it be zeal for the Master's glory that inspired such a misrepresentation of brethren? 'Selfish earnestness!' 'Proud resolve!' 'Making a manageable business of conversion!' 'Intolerant of any recognition of the sovereignty of God!'

'There is, of course, frequent reference to the Spirit, and an acknowledgment of the necessity of His work, but there is, after all, *very little allowed him to do*; and *bustling men* feel and act as if somehow His power was under their control' (pp. 21,22).

Thus we are said to acknowledge the Spirit in words, but 'allow Him nothing to do!' Are we really so far astray as this? 'Bustling men!' 'Acting as if the Spirit's power were under our control!' We plead not guilty.

'Those who are *blindly craving some excitement* may be preparing instruments to be used by some other power than that of the Spirit of the Lord' (p. 22).

We are not conscious of any 'blind craving for excitement.' All has been profound calm amongst us. No fever has prevailed. We are 'preparing instruments' for Satan! We have prayed and striven for the contrary.

'It is terrible to think of *an impenitent people* regarding as a gracious work of God *that which is really not so*, that, under the

67

covert of an imagined mercy, they may remain at ease in their sins, and *congratulate themselves on having been favoured by the Lord, without having to part with their idols'* (p. 22).

We are willing to confess sin, but not because of what we are here charged with,—leading an impenitent people into self-delusion. We should like to be made to feel sins and burdens more. But we are not convinced that such a depth of delusion or such an amount of hypocrisy is to be found in us as is affirmed here. Such charges, if made at all, should be confirmed with evidence, and made with a broken-heartedness and brotherly love which we look for in vain in these pages.

'In the present movement there seems to be little that is allowed of work to the Spirit of the Lord' (p. 22).

'In the prominent teaching *there is no exposure of the total depravity* and the utter spiritual impotence of souls dead in trespasses and sins' (p. 22).

Unless the writer had heard all that was said at all the meetings, he was scarcely entitled to make such a wide statement,—a statement of which I can only say, and say as kindly yet as firmly as I can, that it is *utterly incorrect.* Will the writer prove his assertion, and summon us before the Courts of the Church for such unsoundness and unfaithfulness?

'To face this reality in the light of God's word would be to discover the necessity of the almighty agency of the Holy Ghost. *This cannot be endured'* (pp. 22,23).

We not only can *endure* the discovery of the necessity of the Spirit's work, but we *believe* it, and *preach* it, and *press* it. How such an uncharitable taunt could have been deemed necessary, I am at a loss to see. I am persuaded that there is not one brother connected with the work who does not acknowledge fully and preach boldly the absolute necessity of the Spirit's work. What satisfaction can a Christian man have in speaking thus of his brethren;—in bringing up an evil report against them, who have done him no wrong, and who have done the Church some service, in past days at least, if not in the present work?

'You would *hoodwink their understandings,* and misdirect the movements to which their sense of responsibility urges them'

(p. 23).

We are not aware of 'hoodwinking any man's understanding, or of 'misdirecting their movements.' Among the hundreds of brethren connected with this movement, are there none of whom better things can be said,—things more in accordance with the charity which 'thinketh no evil'? When the pressure of conscience leads one brother to withstand another to the face, he will surely choose words conveying the least possible imputation of improper motives. It is not so here.

'*You hide the true state of things from yourselves as well as from them.* You do so that you may have hope of success' (p. 23).

Indeed we do not. We do our utmost, by prayer and watchfulness and heart-searching, to know the true state of things. Yet we do come short; for 'the heart is deceitful above all things, and desperately wicked.'

'You have *no faith in the Spirit of God.* You cannot bear, therefore, to discover that there is a great work for Him to do; and *you cannot endure to feel dependent on His love,* for you cannot trust in it as the love of God' (p. 23).

Nay, but we have faith in the Spirit of God, say what you will. We do know that there is a great work for Him to do, and we can endure to feel dependent both on His love and power. Why should you doubt us?

'You would fain account the work to be done as not too much for your own power of persuasion; for *you are ambitious of having it to do yourselves, as well as hopeless of having it done by the Lord*' (p. 23).

We would fain put from us all such spiritual ambition as is here imputed to us, so unjustly and with such warmth. We are not hopeless of the Lord's power and willingness; we despair of ourselves, not of Him.

'And yet, *forsooth,* you are the men who have faith, and those who differ from you are the dupes of unbelief. Yes, you are the men of faith; but *yours is faith in men*' (p. 23).

That word 'forsooth' does not read well; it sounds unkindly and unpleasantly in connection with such a serious matter. We never boasted of faith, but have always mourned over our unbelief. As to the bitter words, 'yours is faith in men,' we have nothing to say. The assumption of spiritual superiority is always unbecoming, but specially so when rebuking a brother. I cannot but express my regret that these words should have been written. I have rarely read such an uncalled for censure against brethren, such an unsupported accusation from one who, after all, may perhaps find himself in the wrong. 'Ye know not what manner of spirit ye are of.'

'It does raise one's indignation to hear some men speak of what would conserve to the Spirit of God, His place and work, as a *mere obscuration of the grace of the gospel,* and a fettering of souls in bondage. But it grieves one's heart to know that this is tolerated, and even approved of, by some who ought to be more zealous for the grace and glory of the Lord than to be able to endure it' (p. 25).

I never heard, in all the many addresses and sermons delivered during the past ten months, anything that would warrant such a representation as this. There is not one of us, I am bold to say, who would regard the necessity of the Spirit's work as an obscuration of the grace of the gospel. We know, and believe, and preach, that the gospel is of no effect without the accompanying power of the almighty Spirit; and that in preaching the Spirit's work, broadly, boldly, freely, we do not obscure but enhance the grace of the gospel.

'No care is taken to show, in the light of the doctrine of the cross, how God is glorified in the salvation of a sinner. The *designed overliness* with which the doctrine of sin is stated necessarily leads to this' (p. 25).

The author may not have heard of the care taken for this end, but it is true that this has been done;—yes, done earnestly and constantly. The charge of 'designed overliness' should certainly not have been made.

'Neither teacher nor disciple seem to desiderate aught besides the assurance that salvation can be reached by faith. The gospel seems convenient for man, and that suffices' (p. 25).

What can we do in reference to an unproved charge like this but simply deny it? The sharpness of the words adds very painfully to the seriousness of the misrepresentation.

'How salvation is to the praise of God's glory the one (the teacher) is not anxious to show, the other (the disciple) is not anxious to know. To any unprejudiced observer this must have appeared a marked feature of revival teaching' (pp. 25,26).

Thus the brand of unsound teaching is indiscriminately affixed to all revival work. Have there been no revivals originating in sound teaching? This looks like reprobation of all revivals. Probably it was meant to be so, and seems to indicate that, in the writer's opinion, no revivals can be carried on in which the truth of God is not endangered or obscured.

'Faith, in *the convenient arrangement* for deliverance from danger, is substituted for trust in the Person who glorified God on earth' (p. 26).

I never once heard faith thus dealt with during the whole movement. It was always referred to as connected (1) with a truth, (2) with a testimony, (3) with a promise, (4) with a Person. To remove mystifications connected with faith, which are obscuring the cross in the eye of the anxious, is not to make it void.

'No precaution is offered against a tendency to Antinomianism in those who profess to have believed. Yea, this tendency must be fostered by the teaching given to them' (p. 27)

Very many have been the precautions which we have taken against Antinomianism. In private and in public, in books and by addresses, we have kept this in view, as I well know. To say that we *'foster'* it is somewhat too bad. Our Northern brother's *preconception* that our system leads to this laxity is no proof of the thing.

'Not having respect to the standard of God's law, it is easy for him to imagine that he is without sin. He is taught now that he has nothing to do with the confession of sin, because his sins were long ago disposed of, and that he should not remember them' (p. 27).

We have taught invariably, and with no uncertain sound, 'respect to the standard of God's law.' *We confess sin, and we teach all who hear us to confess it.* How such a charge could have been brought against us I am at a loss to conceive. Any one who has heard the full, large, solemn confessions of sin at our meetings, will be satisfied with the injustice of the accusation.

'As for the corruption of his nature, it never was a trouble to him; and is less likely to be so now than before, since *a delusive peace has drugged his soul to sleep*' (p. 27).

'Never troubled with the corruption of his nature!' Would that our brother had conversed with a few of the awakened! He would have omitted this charge. 'Delusive peace!' How does he know that the peace is delusive? Or is it allowable for him to call a thing evil, but not allowable for us to call it good? 'Drugged his soul to sleep!' How can I answer a charge like this? On what information is the statement made? Is it by intuition or a prophetic gift that this is done? How has he learned so quickly the *secrets* of so many hearts? Had the writer merely spoken of the danger of such evils arising, I should have nothing to say. He is at liberty to affirm this. But when he comes to 'facts' or 'experiences' of which he knows nothing, I am entitled, in self-defence, to *deny the whole charge* from my personal knowledge, and to claim the benefit of full and honest proof. The charge of 'drugging the soul' implies something worse on our part than mistake or ignorance.

'Antinomianism, leading in the first instance to perfectionism, must be the result of the teaching under which he has been trained' (p. 27).

I need hardly remark on this statement; because, after all, it is but the expression of an opinion, not the statement of a fact. The opinion of hundreds of men, sound in the faith, and approved for zeal and sobriety in the Church, is precisely the reverse of that above quoted. Many 'Southrons' think that it is rather the Northern teaching that produces Antinomianism.

'In his leader's prayers he never hears any confession of sin' (p. 27).

I have myself (as I have already stated) heard such full and fervent confessions of sin at Mr. Moody's meetings, and such solemn addresses concerning this at our 'converts'' meetings, that I can give my testimony as to the inaccuracy of the charge. We do confess sin and seek forgiveness; we teach the converts to do the same. I have seldom heard any one cast himself more entirely upon God for pardon and for strength and wisdom than 'the leader.'

'Meetings are multiplied that he may attend them, and crowds are gathered that he may address them. The excitement of his first impressions is thus to be kept up by the bustle of evangelistic service. And what kind of being is he likely to become under such training as this? *A molluscous, flabby creature, without pith or symmetry,* breathing freely only in the heated air of meetings, craving to be *pampered with vapid sentiment,* and so puffed up by foolish flattery as to be in a state of *chronic flatulency, requiring relief in frequent bursts of hymn singing, in spouting addresses* as void of Scripture truth as of common sense, and in *belching flippant questions in the face of all he meets.* Self-examination he discards as *a torture only meant for slaves, humility and watchfulness as troublesome virtues* which the wise will eschew, secret communion with God as a relic of less enlightened and less busy times, and the quiet habitual discharge of home duties in the fear of God as a TAME ROUTINE FOR LEGALISTS' (pp. 27, 28).

These are hard sayings. I did not think that a man of God and a brother in Christ could have so forgotten the brotherhood that there is between us and him. They look like the words of strong human feeling, uttered in the name of the Lord; implying, throughout, a sense of superiority in the writer, entitling him to rebuke and judge his brethren, without any apparent consciousness that he himself stands in need of rebuke and judgment. There are many expressions in the pamphlet which courtesy might have polished, if Christianity did not restrain.

'Others, *strangers to stated spiritual enjoyment* in the means of grace, were longing for some change, some excitement to lift them out of their dullness, and for some bustle in which they might take their share of service. Others still, *who knew no happiness in the house of God, and had no desire for His presence,* would fain that something new were introduced into the mode of service which they felt so jading. The excitement of a revival would be to them a relief' (p. 29).

How this could be known save by Omniscience I do not understand. The judgment here pronounced may not be meant to be infallible, but it is put in such a form as to make one feel that certainly this judge must have had access to the hearts of the hundreds in Edinburgh last November when they came together to seek a revival. They were 'strangers to stated spiritual enjoyment!' How has he been able to 'search their hearts and try their reins'? This is not the judgment of charity. *

'But many there were who merely craved a change,—something to relieve them of the tedium of a routine in which they found no enjoyment *because they were estranged from God*, and who joined in asking this with those who were asking something better. These were the persons disposed to make much of their prayers, and who found it easy to hope just because they had chosen to ask; and *they may have received, though not in mercy, what they sought'* (p. 29).

How could the writer be so sure that many of those who last November

---

* 'The little flock of tender-hearted Christians, scattered throughout his parish, were, at the same time, moved with a sense of the prevalence of sin and the desolations of Zion. They felt an increased concern for the conversion and salvation of sinners, and a deeper interest in the prosperity and enlargement of the kingdom of Christ. They began to be more frequent and earnest in their supplications at a throne of grace for a time of revival—of refreshing from the presence of the Lord. Several little parties of them, by mutual consent, set apart some days for private fasting and prayer, sending up their united supplications to the Hearer of prayer for the downpouring of the Spirit in His awakening and converting influences on sinners around them. They kept several such days *for nearly a twelvemonth* before the commencement of what is generally called "The Revival of Religion in Arran." In these devotional exercises, some of them enjoyed uncommon nearness to God, and great freedom at a throne of grace when pouring out their hearts in earnest supplication for the manifestation of divine power and glory in the sanctuary, especially in the congregation with which they were themselves connected. Their minds were much stirred up to press after these things in secret, and at their fellowship meetings, and also when attending public ordinances.'—*Old Tract*. It was thus that the Christians in Arran prayed for a revival in 1812,—and it was in such a spirit that the Christians in Edinburgh came together in November 1873 to pray for the same.

sought a revival *'merely craved a change to relieve the tedium of a rou-tine,'* that they 'were estranged from God,' and that 'they may have received, THOUGH NOT IN MERCY, what they sought.' These last words almost appal us. We have got answers, it is admitted; yes, but they are *in judgment, not in mercy!* We ourselves, whatever others may think, know the opposite. We can sing of mercy; and the conversion of our children (to say nothing more) *has not been an answer of judgment.* Perhaps the reply would be, that these conversions are delusions of the Evil One!

'In course of time, musical practisings were added to prayer meetings, as preparation for a revival! From both the addresses and the music much was expected when evangelistic deputies arrived' (p. 30).

This charge about 'musical practisings' being 'added to prayer meetings as a preparation for revival' surprises us. Are 'musical practisings' wrong? Are they wrong as a preparation for the weekly worship of the sanctuary? Where is the sin of their being adopted in order to the better service of a revival meeting? Is it meant that they were mere amusement? or that they were substitutes for prayer and preaching? The previous 'practising,' in order to the more perfect singing at a gathering of some two or three thousand people, seems to us not at all out of place.

'A system of doctrine that ignored those aspects of the truth which are most offensive to "the natural man," and that, while offering something that seemed plausible to an unenlightened conscience, seemed to conserve the old heart's imagined independence of the sovereign and almighty grace of God, and by ignoring repentance preserved to it its idols. The gospel, modified to suit the taste of unrenewed men, was welcome. The recommendations of it, given by men of influence, tended to put down suspicion, and to induce the public to receive it as "the gospel of the grace of God." The new style of teaching made it seem such an easy thing to be a Christian' (p. 30).

Our 'system of doctrine' is said to 'ignore those aspects of truth which are most offensive to the natural man;' to 'conserve the old heart's imagined independence of the sovereign and almighty grace of God;' to 'ignore repentance.' It is a gospel 'modified to suit the taste of unrenewed men,' yet 'recommended by men of influence.' It is clear that we of the South, though called evangelical, are not unlike the Moderates of old. The above is a huge array of charges. In reply, I ask for some *proof.* Am I not entitled to make this request? What is the *system* thus condemned? We certainly *mean* to preach and teach such a system as the Shorter Catechism contains. It would be well if our opposers would point out wherein we deny or diverge from the articles of that Compendium of Doctrine. We are not aware of doing so. Would they also state explicitly what *their* gospel is, and wherein it is glad tidings to sinners?

'All who say they are converted were set to work. Any one *who can tongue it deftly* can take a part; he requires neither knowledge nor experience. The excitement is kept up by the bustle of public service' (p. 30).

'Who can *tongue it* deftly!' Surely this is language too low for such an occasion. It does not indicate that spiritual calmness which one assuming the position of reprover of his brethren should have striven to exercise. 'The wrath of man worketh not the righteousness of God.'

'A season apart, to be alone with God, a solemn time for careful counting of the cost, has from Christ the double recommendation of His example and of His precept, *but is desired neither by nor for these so-called converts* ' (pp. 30,31).

To be alone with God '*is desired neither by nor for these so-called converts!*' In earnestly denying this statement I restrain myself, lest I should be betrayed into the same spirit of censoriousness as is exhibited here. How could Dr. Kennedy know (unless by discernment of spirits) that retirement 'is not desired either by or for these converts?' He will not surely say, 'Wot ye not that such a man as I can certainly divine?' May these words yet be repented of and forgiven! He who knows all things knows how untrue they are.

'Even prayer meetings are converted into *factories of sensation.* Brief prayers and brief addresses to the stroke of hammer or the toll of bell; silent prayers; hymns, which often contain a considerable amount of nonsense, and occasionally of something worse, sung to the strains of an organ; and a chance to address or pray given to any one who chooses to rise and speak,—such are the arrangements of the new prayer meeting' (p. 34).

This is keen language, breathing anything but charity towards the brethren. Their prayer meetings are 'factories of sensation!' I can testify that they are not so, but calm, sober, solemn meetings. The 'stroke of the hammer,' the 'toll of the bell,' the 'nonsense-hymns,' the 'organ strains,'—these are flung upon the canvas to make up a picture, as unlike the original as any caricature can be imagined to be.

We are most willing to listen to one whose voice we have often heard with unfeigned pleasure; but we cannot accept his judgement as final, or as at all binding on our consciences. He has written many hard things against his brethren, which we trust he will yet regret and retract. His charges are very sweeping; and as he names no names, each Christian man who has taken part in the work condemned feels that he himself is meant. I am quite willing to bear the imputations laid on us with all patience, and I can excuse what I must call the serious inaccuracies scattered throughout; * but I cannot account for the *acerbity*. Zeal for the glory of God does not usually engender bitterness, or expel charity from the soul or from the pen.

---

* At pp. 18,19 we read: 'Why raise up your sins again, to think of and to confess them? their leading teacher said to them; for they were disposed of nearly two thousand years ago. Just believe this, and go home and sing and dance.' Something like this was one day said in the Assembly Hall, but it was not by 'the leading teacher,' or by any of those connected with the work. Whoever said it spoke unadvisedly with his lips. Yet how often did Luther *write* thus! Many times over we find stronger statements than the above in his *Commentary on Galatians*. Here is a specimen: 'What is this to me, O law, that thou accusest me, and sayest that I have committed many sins? Indeed I grant that I have committed many sins; yea, and still commit sins daily without number. *This toucheth me nothing. I am now deaf, and cannot hear.* Therefore thou talkest to me in vain, for I am dead unto thee. If thou wilt needs dispute with me touching my sins, get thee to my flesh and members, my servants; teach them, exercise and edify them. But trouble not me, conscience, I say, who am already forgiven, and have nothing to do with thee, for I am dead to thee and now live to Christ' (*Com. on Gal.* ch. ii. ver. 19). Certainly Luther did write rashly, and others have spoken no less so. But Luther wrought a blessed work for all that. In reference to the words ascribed to Mr. Moody, I am glad to be able to give the testimony of my much esteemed friend, Mr. Fairbairn of Newhaven: 'I heard them spoken in the meeting last winter by one whose name I know not. But this I am ready to declare, that *these words, or anything like them, were never spoken in my hearing by Mr Moody. I heard him often, and I never heard him utter a word that was inconsistent with*

We have been at much pains all along to prevent excrescences, to preserve calmness, to present the truth of God, to guard against error, to watch over the work in every possible way. That work has been kept in the hands of well-known ministers and elders of maturity, of soundness in the faith, of unblemished character; men whom the Churches have honoured and trusted. And if opponents can suggest any further suitable safeguards, we shall be truly happy to adopt them. I may safely say this, however, that I believe there never has been a spiritual movement in our land where *so many precautions were taken against everything improper, unsound, and hollow, and where so many tried servants of God of every sound Protestant name have been gathered together to carry it on in such ways as might most hinder the growth of evil, and best contribute to the promotion of good, both in doctrine and in life.*

Even during the two months in Edinburgh when our American friends were with us, hundreds of trusted men, ministers and others, were daily present to assist in the work; and this co-operation was of the closest and most confidential kind. Every day (at first) our large committee met for consultation, when everything connected with the work and its progress was freely talked over, and plans devised for greater efficiency, or, it might be, greater safety. The means adopted may not invariably commend themselves to those outside, but they were means devised by honest Christian men, men of name and standing, after prayerful consultation and anxious thought, for the promotion of what they believed to be a work of God. There might be imperfections in the proceedings; the harmonium and the hymn-singing might not commend themselves to some; but still, discounting these 'blots,' as some will call them, did there not remain enough of excellence behind to warrant our rejoicing in the work as genuine? We had

---

Scripture truth. I bear willing testimony to the blessed effects among my own people by Moody's teaching and Sankey's singing; and I know of at least one sorrowful soul who never either heard the one or the other, but was mightily helped even by imperfect reports in her passage through the dark valley and across the river.... This note is an expression of my high estimate of Moody and Sankey, of little value in itself except as coming from one who in *all this movement has been very jealous on the side of orthodoxy.*' Besides the above testimony, a letter from Mr. Moody himself is now before me, denying that he ever uttered these words, 'Go home, sing and dance,' and affirming that when he did speak of its not being needful to bring sin continually back, he was speaking to *Christians,* and warning them against bringing up sin continually, *as if it had not been forgiven.*

done what in us lay, as true men, to carry on the work of God; and it is hard to blame us for not making it perfect; for not preventing the possibility of the 'wayside,' or the 'stony-ground,' or the 'thorny-ground' hearer. The Lord's parable speaks only of one-fourth of the seed as bearing fruit; so that even if three-fourths of the work turned out ill, should we not rejoice in the remaining fourth?

In pronouncing the work authentic, we do not 'lay claim to inspiration' (p. 13). We simply declare, that what we have seen or heard during the past twelve months appears to us who have watched and tested it day by day to be as like a true work of God as any that we have seen or heard of. Let others judge for themselves upon our report. We claim no inspiration. But this we may say, that if nothing short of inspiration entitles us to affirm the truth of the work at an early stage, then nothing short of this will entitle us to pronounce upon it at any time or stage, seeing no amount of evidence nor length of time can prevent an uninspired man from being deceived in his estimate or in his evidence. Probation, how ever long, can never preclude the possibility of deception. And yet, though we do not lay claim to the gifts of the Ross-shire men of God in other days, yet we do claim the right, nay, insist on the duty, of pronouncing a verdict according to the nature and amount of *the evidence before us at the time*. The truth is, we cannot help doing so, especially if we be ministers. For we have to deal regularly with those who seek admission to the table of the Lord. What are we to do with these applicants? Suppose sixty come to us before a communion, professing a spiritual change, and giving all the evidence that can be given up to that time; suppose we examine them as closely as we are able, again and again, both as to their knowledge and their conversion to God; and suppose, after this careful examination and credible profession, we admit them as communicants,—are we laying claim to inspiration in so doing? Shall we refuse admission in such a case after we have satisfied ourselves, so far as it is possible for one to judge who is not a discerner of spirits, that they are what they profess to be, true disciples of the Lord? Must we wait for *a certainty equal to inspiration* before we admit them;—and, in admitting them, affirm that a genuine and extensive work of God has been going on amongst us? In Edinburgh and throughout all Scotland, during the past year, ministers of all denominations have been doing this. They have been examining and admitting many thousands of applicants for communion; and in doing so they have been, consciously or unconsciously (yet without claim to inspiration), declaring that a notable work of God has been going on in the land. Time will test the work; the precious will be separated from the vile; the love of many may wax cold; but meanwhile *necessity is laid on us* to say that, as Christian ministers, we are persuaded that the Spirit of God (and not Satan, as the pamphlet suggests) has been working amongst us.

Here, then, are our witnesses,—the ministers of Scotland. We can call them by hundreds, and they will bear testimony. Is this testimony not to be believed? If not, *what* is to be believed, or *who*?

There is another class of witnesses, no less credible and important,—the Sabbath-school teachers of Scotland, amounting to thousands. They can tell of the wonderful changes in their scholars, such as they never saw before; changes which betoken the Spirit's hand, and indicate genuine renovation of heart. Will the opponents of the work take these witnesses and examine them before casting discredit on it? Surely, if their hearts are sad and 'strained to breaking,' they will be anxious to know the truth, so that they may form no false judgment on a work which so many of their brethren believe to be the work of God.

There is yet another class of witnesses whom I would summon,— the *parents* of Scotland. One of the remarkable things about this work, especially in Edinburgh and Glasgow, is that so many of the children of pious parents have been gathered in. What changes in families have been accomplished! What different households do we now see! There are hundreds of fathers and mothers who could come forward as witnesses to tell of the fruit among their children. Must no parent rejoice over the conversion of a child because, perhaps, the change may not be permanent? He may rejoice with trembling, but surely he ought to rejoice. Shall he weep over a son's profligacy, and not give thanks for that child's return from the error of his ways? Must joy like this be called 'blind sanguineness' (p. 14), and must we be told that 'a favourable verdict at that stage no man *not a prophet has any right to pronounce*' (p. 13). 'This is a hard saying; who can hear it?' The work of God on earth, then, can never be known with certainty at all, by minister, by teacher, or by parent; for lapse of time, though it may *increase the probabilities,* never can produce certainty, unless the prophetic gift and discerning of spirits can be exercised. No multiplication of uncertainties can produce certainty, and the 'unfavourable verdict' must continue to the last. In connection with the work among the *young,* I could say much; but I must forbear. Hundreds of these have been drawn out of the gay world and from youthful follies, as well as from more open sins. They have walked hitherto in the fear of the Lord. But what can they say when reading this pamphlet?

These words come in here with solemn force: 'Take heed that ye offend not one of these little ones that believe on me!' Yet no one, I believe, will regret more than its author, if this pamphlet shall prove a stumbling-block in the way of the least of these little ones.

We have taken, I have said, all the pains we could to prevent the evil and promote the good. We have been very jealous for the good name of the work, and of Him for whom we claim it. We have examined each applicant singly. We have recorded their names and addresses. We have corresponded with their ministers, and sent their names to these ministers, that the professed converts may be known, and watched over, and taught. We have subdivided our city into districts, and appointed Christian men and women to go after all these professed subjects of the change. We have distributed sound books amongst them. We have gathered them together every Monday evening at eight o'clock, to be taught by the trustiest of our ministers and elders. We get reports from our visitors, and we ourselves have become acquainted with the greatest number of them. Is there anything more that could be done by us in order to ascertain the genuineness of the work, or to protect it from lapsing into either delusion or inconsistency? We have, week after week, preached the truth of God to these 'converts;' we have sent them to the study of their Bibles and to the company of the godly. We still keep our eye upon them in love and faithfulness, knowing the perils to which they are exposed, and the many that are waiting for their halting. We are certainly, then, entitled to a respectful hearing from our brethren, and we should have expected to be spared the fearful imputations made against us in this pamphlet; for there is hardly any one kind of evil that can be supposed to occur in such a case that is not here laid to our charge. *

---

* My much-esteemed brother, Mr. J. H. Wilson, suggests to me such things as the following concerning the work:—The tree is known by its fruits. Some of these fruits have been, love for and study of the Bible to an extraordinary extent, so that there has been a demand for Bibles such as has seldom been known. There is a teachable spirit among the converts; a tender conscience, seeking to know duty; love of the ordinary means of grace; honour and appreciation of a stated ministry; eagerness to bring others under its influence; love of prayer, private as well as public, so that our prayer meetings (conducted in the old way) are greatly increased; our session meetings and deacons' court meetings turned into prayer meetings. Then there have been remarkable changes in families. Family worship begun; gaiety given up; balls and parties refused; prodigal sons brought back; profane swearing lessened; the idle beginning to work; medical students offering themselves to the work of the Lord; many a dying testimony to these meetings;

We have done what we could to prevent its being a shallow, a superficial, or a sentimental work; and the use of hymns and instruments is no proof that it *must be so*. These appendages may have been in use and the work may be real after all. We have preached both law and gospel, both sovereignty and grace; we have endeavoured to search as well as to comfort; to throw down as well as to build up; to declare the terrors of the Lord as well as the riches of grace. And it is as unjust as it is unbrotherly to charge us with the neglect of the 'weightier matters' of either law or gospel.

Dr. Kennedy says:

'No pains are taken to present the character and claims of God as Lawgiver and Judge, and no indication given of a desire to bring souls in self-condemnation to accept the punishment of their iniquity' (p. 17).

I totally disclaim this. It is wholly inaccurate. We have taken pains to do the very thing which he charges us with omitting. What can I more say? Let the above imputation be proved by credible witnesses, not asserted upon hearsay.

Dr. Kennedy says:

'It ignores the sovereignty and power of God in the dispensation of His grace' (p. 21).

Can I do more than simply contradict this? It does not ignore the sovereignty and power of God. If the writer had said that it did so *in his judgment*, I should not have noticed this; but when the charge is put in this broad way, I must simply but decidedly repel it. We believe in these truths as firmly as does the writer. *

---

communicants greatly increased, both in quantity and quality. These results have been even in many places where Mr. Moody has never been.

* The reader will remember the way in which good men of the last century, such as the Erskines and others, spoke against Whitefield as an emissary of the Evil One, and of the work of Cambuslang, Kilsyth, etc. as the work of the devil. A day of fasting was appointed to mourn over the delusions and false doctrines connected with that movement, and about as hard things were said of it as are now of the present work. Yet Whitefield was a man of God, and doing the work of God, though belonging to the Church of England, and using hymns and organs when it suited him.

Dr. Kennedy remarks:

'No care is taken to show, in the light of the doctrine of the cross, how God is glorified in the salvation of a sinner' (p. 25).

I must just repeat, what I have said in regard to many previous statements, that this is not the case. Why we should be accused of this we know not. Times without number have we endeavoured 'to show, in the light of the doctrine of the cross, how God is glorified in the salvation of the sinner.' We may have failed in that which we aimed at. We may not have done this so effectively as some of our brethren would. But we have, nevertheless, endeavoured to do it fully and faithfully, according to the ability which God has given us. Some, we doubt not, do it better than we; still we have done what we could, in the course of (in some of us) a lengthened ministry, to show, in the light of the cross, how God is glorified in the sinner's conversion. How could we preach the cross at all if we did not preach this? How could we tell of salvation if we did not tell it in connection with the glory of God?

In the seven epistles to the Churches of Asia we have a specimen of how we should deal with the erring. The Master is showing the disciple how to speak to brethren who have gone astray, or become cold, or departed from the truth, or forgotten Himself. I think that if the present author had written in the spirit of these epistles, he would have been lovingly listened to by those whom he blames so sharply. I know that we should take reproof, in whatever tones it may be spoken; but the continuous language of judgment,—severe and, as it seems to us, unjust,—is somewhat hard to bear. Even had the words of this pamphlet come to us from more venerable lips, we should have been repelled, if not irritated. But when they come from a peccable brother like ourselves, and when we contrast them with the calm, kind tone of the Master in speaking to His fallen Churches, we are troubled not a little, and are ready, I will not say to resent, but at least to repel, both the language and the tone. Grant that we are worse than Ephesus or Sardis or Laodicea, we might have been dealt with by the servant as the Master dealt with these. With what divine delicacy does He begin His reproof!—'Nevertheless, I have somewhat against thee.' He says all the good he can of them before he utters one word of censure. And that censure, when it comes, how tender! How fitted to disarm either resistance or resentment; and to bring conviction calmly home to the apostate Church or to the fallen saint!

Very many of the expressions in this pamphlet remind us of the Lord's words to these Churches: 'I know thy works.' We feel that the servant is judging us as only the Master can do. Only He who searcheth the hearts and trieth the reins, and whose eyes are as a flaming fire, was entitled to write to us as our brother has done. The Lord was warranted in saying to us, 'Thou art neither cold nor hot,' and in charging us with being instruments of Satan in carrying on this work; with being 'intolerant of any recognition of the sovereignty of God;' with 'blindly craving some excitement;' with 'not being able to endure the necessity of the almighty agency of the Holy Ghost;' with being 'ambitious to do God's work ourselves;' with only 'having faith in men;' with 'discarding self-examination as a torture only meant for slaves;' with being 'strangers to stated spiritual enjoyment;' with 'knowing no happiness in the house of God, and having no desire for His presence;' with 'not desiring to be alone with God, either for ourselves or the converts.' Yes, the Lord, the Searcher of hearts, might have said these things to us; but how a man like ourselves, whatever his attainments may be, without the Master's omniscience and without the Master's love, could have ventured to say them, we do not understand.

Perhaps he who thus 'searches our hearts and tries our reins' in this pamphlet may say that he did not mean these imputations for all his brethren, but only for some. But he makes no distinction. And even if he did, would it mend the matter? Would it justify him in thus saying things against any professing Christian which only the Heart-searcher could discover? If a distinction is to be made between those who conducted these meetings, it would be better that this were distinctly notified, and the men pointed out. As the pamphlet now reads, all who took the responsibility of these meetings, or took part in them, are equally guilty. 'The leader' may perhaps be the worst, but all those who associated themselves with him, and who 'relieved their chronic flatulence with frequent bursts of hymn-singing,' are equally incriminated. Surely, if the impossibility of knowing our hearts did not preclude these evil surmisings, the charity that thinketh no evil might have forbidden them. 'One is your Master, even Christ, and all ye are brethren.'

Would that we could imitate the spirit of these matchless epistles without presuming to act on their inspired discernment! They are Christ's last legacies of love to His Church on earth, His last specimens of counsel and reproof. I feel how little I myself, in this reply, have been able to imitate the Master's spirit; how much of earthly feeling has, often unconsciously, thrown itself into the argument; and how often undue warmth, that looks like zeal, may have given a sharper edge to sentences than should have been. I know how difficult it is to write even one page of controversy without preferring victory to truth, and how little at times one is sensible of the strength or keenness of the language which flows from his pen; the unconscious wish to wound so often overmastering the desire to conciliate. But as one who had been much engaged not only with the present movement, but with most of the former ones which have been often spoken against, I wished to bear my testimony to the excellence of the work at present assailed, and to repel the evil reports which have been brought against it; and this not in order to wound a much-esteemed brother, but to vindicate what I believe to be the truth and the work of God.

But whether I may have been able to write with sufficient calmness or not, I feel constrained to say what I have said; and even apart from the wrong that has been done to the work of which we are witnesses, there is something in the spirit which pervades this pamphlet which we cannot but feel to be alike unjust and unmeet. We are ministers of Christ as well as the writer; some of us are of older standing than he; and though years may not always teach, yet, in the present case, we are constrained to say that we cannot accept the adverse verdict thus so unsparingly given against us, nor admire the confidence with which it has been pronounced.

I have still one or two further remarks. If this pamphlet represent fairly the gospel of the North, then there is a wide difference between North and South. There is 'another gospel' somewhere. Whether it is connected with the 'hyper-evangelism' of the present movement, I let others judge. We may dread 'hyper-evangelism;' but is 'hyper-Calvinism' innocuous? If the former is to be charged with drawing many who are not drawn of the Father, the latter may with more truth be chargeable with repelling many to whom the Saviour says, 'Come unto me.'

I have heard the opinion of some concerning this work, that even if there be no error accompanying it, and no unscriptural methods adopted, still the result will be a sentimental religion, an effeminate Christianity.

I cannot bring myself to believe this. I have seen much less sensation about this than about former revivals. The men who have conducted it are men to whose character no effeminacy belongs, and in whose preaching sentimentalism has no place. There has been enough of manly vigour and robust character in the agents to free them from the suspicion of fostering, consciously or unconsciously, either the sickly or the hollow in religion. They do not suit their addresses to the susceptible or the weak.

The pamphlet predicts that the offspring of this awakening will be 'a *molluscous flabby* creature,'—'breathing freely only in the heated air of meetings,'—'craving to be pampered with vapid sentiment,'—'in a state of *chronic flatulency*, requiring relief in frequent bursts of hymn-singing, in spouting addresses as void of Scripture as of common sense, and in *belching flippant questions* in the face of ALL he meets.' I am persuaded that these predictions will not be verified. Yet I would not be over sure of the issue even of the most blessed movement, when I remember how Ephesus went back, and Sardis grew cold, and Laodicea became lukewarm.

I am satisfied that the teaching given is not fitted to produce such evil results. It has not been perfect, for the teachers are but men. It may have been not according to the standard of some; but it is the teaching of the Westminster Confession and the Shorter Catechism; and seldom have I heard the doctrine of the divine purpose in election more unreservedly and unequivocally stated than by Mr. Moody. The addresses were those of clear-headed, warm-hearted men,—of various gifts, no doubt, for there were hundreds of them,—men whose great aim was to declare the mind of God, and not to suit their teaching to the convenience of the sinner. The manner and tone and substance all betokened a robust and manly Christianity. The words were of-tentimes of the most searching kind, going deep down into the con-science of the sinner, and sweeping away every refuge of lies. There was no trifling with sin, no undervaluing of holiness, no ignoring of the law, no uncertain sound of the trumpet, either as to the present condemnation of the unconverted or as to the wrath to come which they were treasuring up for themselves; and that word 'repent'—how I have heard it ring through the Assembly Hall in the ears of thou-sands! There was no prophesying smooth things, no soothing the soul to sleep with Arminian or Antinomian opiates, but bold proclamation both of the law and of the grace,—the law that condemns, and the grace that saves. 'I love those that thunder out the word,' said Whitefield; 'the Christian world is in a deep sleep, and needs to be awaked.' Whitefield would have rejoiced to hear the tones and the words that day by day woke up the gathered multitudes of Edinburgh.

I may say, without going beyond the mark, that since the work began, in November 1873, there cannot have been much fewer than a thousand meetings of all kinds in the Assembly Hall, which was the great centre of all our operations at Edinburgh. Most of those ministers connected with the work have been present at these meetings,—some a hundred times, some two hundred, some five hundred, some six or eight hundred. I am not aware that Dr. Kennedy was present at one of these central meetings, in which the work was mainly carried on. It was certainly, then, somewhat incautious in him to affirm that certain doctrines were never taught at these meetings. He who was not present at any declares that they were *not* taught; we who were present at hundreds of them declare *that they were taught.* Who is to be believed? We say that the doctrine at these meetings was altogether in harmony with the Shorter Catechism; for we heard it with our ears, from Mr. Moody and others;—*nay, we taught it ourselves.* Are we to credit the statement of one man, who was not present, in opposition to the declarations of hundreds who were present,—present hundreds of times,—and who heard not only the thoroughly Calvinistic teaching of Scottish brethren, but the no less Calvinistic teaching of him who is once and again in this pamphlet called 'their leader.' 'I speak as unto wise men; judge ye what I say.'

The work is shallow, say some, and the teaching superficial. That there has been no shallow work and no superficial teaching I will not affirm. But I object to the way in which that word 'depth' has been used by those who have stood aloof from the movement, and who justify their suspicions by declaring that the whole thing 'wants depth.' I would that these objectors had visited the despised 'inquiry room,' and seen but the tenth part of what some of us have witnessed. They would have gone away satisfied that though there might be stony-ground hearers among these inquiring ones, yet, so far as one could judge of the most, there was no lack of depth. Deep conviction of sin was there; the sense of eternal danger was there; the dread of the divine wrath was there; and the bitter question was put, 'Men and brethren, what shall we do?' There were no outcries; nothing more audible than the sob, or more visible than the tear. There were no prostrations or convulsions, such as were seen in Ireland fourteen years ago, and in Arran fifty years ago. There were no screams or loud wailings, such as were heard in the awakenings forty years ago. There were no passionate appeals to feeling, and no wild words of terror speaking only to the human fears of the natural man. These things were unknown. For nearly a year now has the work gone on without any such excrescences or blemishes. Human feeling has been kept back, human eloquence has played no part; the words of God, fresh from His own book, have been read, and reiterated, and enforced.

In Shepherd's well-known work, *The Sound Believer*, now more than 200 years old, we have statements like the following:—'More are drawn to Christ under the sense of a dead blind heart than by all sorrows, humiliations, and terrors.' I notice this because in the revivals of 1839, 1840, 1841, which are spoken of by some as being so much deeper than the present, I knew several who were brought under very awful convictions, and in whom what was apparently a very deep work went on. Yet they did not stand above a year or so; while many others, in whom the terrors were far less, and the work apparently more superficial, stood well, some of them having already 'fallen asleep,' and some remaining steadfast to this day. It is better for us not to fix a certain process through which all must pass before we will own them to be Christians. The work of the Spirit is too secret as well as too varied for us. We cannot lay down rules concerning it.

Prayer has been made without ceasing; and still that solemn noon meeting goes on, with its many hundreds, day by day, and its various requests pouring in from burdened or anxious hearts. We seek to pray and not to faint. Prayer in the closet, prayer in the family, prayer in the congregation,—these are things on which we have laid much stress. God hears the cry of the needy; and such are we. 'Silent prayer' is no new thing. Those who look back into former days will remember how Robert M'Cheyne has sometimes stopped and called for a few minutes of silent prayer. They will remember how William Burns used occasionally to take out his watch, and while calling on God's people to pray silently, say to the unconverted, 'I give you two minutes to close with Christ.' Right or wrong, the practice is no new thing, as many of us have known during the past forty years. And why should there not be silent prayer? Am I to be hindered from lifting up my soul to God silently, and making request for things which, it may be, have been omitted from the public prayer? Why may I not, as a minister, be allowed to say, 'Let us now for a few minutes suspend our uttered prayer and praise, and each one lift up his heart straight to God in his own words and way'? *

---

* Would Dr. Kennedy prohibit us from praying silently while we are seated at the Lord's table during the time of communicating, when every voice is hushed? His words imply this, affirming as they do that the closet is the place for silent and secret prayer, and therefore there ought to be nothing of this in the house of God, either before, or during, or after sermon. Thus I should be prohibited from lifting up my soul to God during the sermon, even to ask a blessing on what I

'The *silent prayer,* what is it? It is secret prayer, and therefore ought to be prayer in secret. It must be *secret,* just because
it is *silent.* And where is it engaged in? In the closet? No; it
was Christ who directed it to be there. There are other leaders
now, and they direct that it should be in open assembly. Christ
would have men, when they pray secretly, to enter their closet
and shut the door. Now it must be done so that those who do it
"may be seen of men." And this device, so directly opposed to
the mind of Christ, is lauded as if nothing could be better. And
it is becoming the habit now of worshippers as they enter the
house of God. They assume, before the eyes of hundreds, the
attitude of prayer, to do in the public assembly what Christ directed to be done in the closet. If they intended this as a public confession of their sin in neglecting prayer in their closet,
such confession would not be at all uncalled for if duly made.
They who forget to do it where Christ required it to be done are
the persons most likely to do it where it can only be a bit of will-
worship and formality' (p. 34).

Because Christ has bidden me pray in the *closet,* am I to have no
secret or silent prayer anywhere else?—by the road, on the mountain,
or in the field? If I happen to come into the sanctuary before the hour
of worship, am I not to pray in silence and secret, because Christ has
commanded secret prayer to be in the closet? This objection certainly is peculiar, and does not commend itself to the simple mind. But
the way in which the argument is put is more unbecoming than the
argument itself; the sarcasm is sadly misplaced, though it is intended to be very keen. Let me repeat it. 'Where is it engaged in? In the
*closet? No; it was Christ who directed it to be there. There are other
leaders now, and they direct that it should be in open assembly!'* Must
all silent prayer be closet prayer, and all closet prayer silent? *May we
never lift up our hearts to God silently in the sanctuary?* If we do so,
must it be 'to be seen of men'? The reasoning in the above passage is,
to say the least, very inconclusive. Might I not call it a specimen of

---

am hearing. Our Directory for Public Worship, in prohibiting those who *come in
late* from engaging in these private devotions, takes for granted that those who
come in early may do so. They must either pray silently or read the Bible. Let
them do either rather than talk to their neighbour or gaze around. A silent minute
also at the close is better than the slamming of doors and rushing out ere the
Amen is well concluded.

'closetism'? The way in which it is put is certainly fitted to wound, but not so certainly to convince.

The 'inquiry meetings' are no new things, and it is unreasonable to blame the present movement because of them. Some of us still remember well the crowded inquiry meetings in Dundee and Perth, as well as elsewhere, now nearly forty years ago. That they have always been soberly conducted I will not undertake to say. That they are right and proper in themselves I have no doubt. Those who remember the crowds pressing into the session-room at St. Peter's and St Leonard's, and who call to mind the earnest, solemn, loving faces of Robert M'Cheyne and John Milne and William Burns, will not be disposed lightly to find fault with them. I cannot expect Dr. Kennedy to see any force in this, for he does not believe in these former revivals any more than in the present one. Nor do I mean the above statement as an argument; I merely remind my brethren of other days, not less blessed than this day of ours, when these inquiry meetings were welcomed by the best and godliest of our ministers. The Moderator's room, attached to the Assembly Hall, has been of late our inquiry room in Edinburgh; and the scenes which we have witnessed there have been solemn beyond description, yet marked by the utmost propriety and order.

As to open meetings, I shall say little. If we threw open our Sabbath service, I should feel the force of the reasoning at p. 34. But it is only our weekly prayer meeting that is thrown open. Are there no open meetings in the North? Dr. Kennedy thus describes a fellowship meeting:

'At first only communicants were present, but latterly *admission became indiscriminate.* The minister presides, and after prayer, praise, and the reading of a portion of Scripture, he calls *on any one who is anxious to propose a question* to the meeting to do so. This call is responded to by some man, who rises, mentions a passage of Scripture describing some feature of the Christian character, and expresses his desire to ascertain the marks of those whom the passage describes, and the various respects in which they may differ from merely nominal Christians' (*Days of the Fathers,* pp. 88, 89).

'On Friday, the day of self-examination, the only public service is in the open air. A large crowd is gathered. "In the tent" there are several godly ministers. The service is that of a fellowship meeting, such as has already been described, but now with special reference to the solemn duties of a communion Sabbath. There are two questions proposed successively to secure variety. Strangers only are called to speak, and even of these only "the flower," for there are so many. Not fewer than thirty will have spoken before the service is over. Blessed indeed to many souls have these "Friday meetings" been' (*Ib.* p. 117).

'On Friday the difficulty in these days would be to select, and not as now to find, "men;" so many would be present who were qualified to speak, and who would be acceptable to their hearers. Each one who was called to speak, knowing this, and unwilling to occupy the time of another, was invariably concise' (*Days of the Fathers,* p. 240).

That these were 'open meetings' is evident from the statement just cited, that the presiding minister 'calls on *any one who is anxious to propose a question* to the meeting to do so.'

I ask the reader's attention to Dr. Kennedy's description of an open meeting in the North, that I may contrast it with his description of an open meeting in the South:—

'The fellowship meeting was a very early product of the vital Christianity of the Highlands. It arose spontaneously out of the lively feeling pervading the first groups of believers there. We cannot conceive of a party of exercised Christians met together without some converse regarding the fruits and evidences of true godliness. Such converse would naturally arise if there was any unsuspecting interchange of thoughts in their intercourse. One of them would be sure to have his doubts and difficulties; these he would state to his brethren, and they, from the word of God and their own experience, would endeavour to afford him suitable counsel and comfort. Finding such converse to be edifying, and remembering that Christians are exhorted to comfort and to edify one another, what would be more likely than that they should set apart seasons for that duty, that He who gave the counsel might have to record the fact, "even as also ye do"? In order to conduct the exercise in an orderly way, what would be more likely than that they should choose him whom they accounted the most advanced among them to preside over them, and that he should ask each one who could do so to speak to the question in course. Thus the fellowship meetings would be at last set up. Why should not the minister then adopt it, and by taking the direction into his own hands, do all he could to provide for its being conducted "decently and in order"? And this is just the story of the rise and establishment of the Highland Fellowship Meeting. It was the product not of the peculiar natural temperament of Highlanders, but of the lively spiritual feeling of Christians, fostered by the warm brotherly love that prevailed in the days of its origin' (*Ib.* pp. 130, 131).

Now let us turn to the following sentence from the present pamphlet:—

'The device of "open meetings," what of it? It is simply ceasing to take care that, in the worship of God, "all things be done decently and in order;" and giving the place to those who have conceit and tongue, and nought beside, which ought to be filled by those who in honour prefer others to themselves, and who seek grace to "serve with reverence and godly fear" (pp. 34,35).

The open meetings of the North are glowingly painted, and I would not say one word of detraction. They were the gatherings of the godly. But an open meeting in the South is 'a device;' a 'ceasing to take care that all things are done decently and in order;' a 'giving place to those who have *conceit* and *tongue* (!), and *nought beside*' (!). What an untrustworthy race we 'Southrons' are! All we do seems evil in the eyes of the North!

I have little to say as to the organ. I do not desire it, and I see no advantage in it. But after all, it was a mere appendage to the proceedings,—and a very small one. Its presence surely could not vitiate the whole work. We have not introduced it into our church services. We prefer the 'voice of the great congregation.' But I decline here to discuss the question of instrumental music.

As to the hymns, I admit that many of them are feeble enough, some worse than feeble,—nearly as bad as our paraphrases, though none of them containing the bald Arminianism which some of these paraphrases give vent to, or the vapid rhymes, meant, no doubt, for poetry, which no one can venture to sing. Dr. Kennedy would do good service to the Free Church if he would in the Church Courts fearlessly attack these relics of Moderatism. To assail feeble hymns outside the Church, and to leave untouched far worse hymns within, is neither consistent nor brave.

I have heard objections to the 'all-day' meeting; yet I cannot say that I have felt their force. In former years these protracted seasons were precious. My readers will remember the 'all-night' meeting at Shotts, before the memorable Monday. They may have heard, too, of the 'all-night' meetings at Kilsyth and Dundee. But here is one from Ross-shire, recorded by Mr. Kennedy:—

'In many instances these prayer meetings have been protracted all night. So sensible were the people of the presence of the Lord, that they could not forsake the place where they enjoyed it; and they found "the joy of the Lord" a sweet substitute for sleep' (pp. 117, 118).

Of unsound doctrine I have heard nothing. That extreme statements may have been made, and one-sided views of truth occasionally exhibited, I might admit; and in doing so I am only admitting what the best and soundest of our ministers will confess as having sometimes been done by themselves. The imperfections of infirm instruments cannot but show themselves at times, especially in days of unusual earnestness.

Of the hasty or premature announcement of conversions, I would only say again, what I have said of other objections, that it is unfair to bring forward a charge against the recent movement which applies equally to former awakenings. In all the awakenings which I remember there was this tendency; and I have never concealed my reluctance to pronounce a judgement on individuals or on a movement till at least some evidence had been given. But then mark how the matter stands as to this. After the awakening last winter, the communion came on in our different Churches. The number applying for admission to the table was in some cases four-fold, in some six-fold, what it used to be. The numbers varied from, perhaps, ten to eighty, all professing to have found the Lord. What were we to do? Were we to grant or refuse admission? Were we not to believe their deeply-touching narratives of passing from darkness to light? Were we not to accept their professions as real, taking what amount of evidence we could have? We were. And doing so, we could not help pronouncing judgment on the cases, and on the movement itself. We were not infallible; but we did what we could to sift each applicant, and to satisfy ourselves that he had undergone a vital change. There was nothing hasty about this. We could not do otherwise. And when all the different ministers came to number up their new communicants, was it wrong for us to take the sum, and to give thanks that so many hundreds had turned from the world to the service of the living God?

As to the use of 'laymen' in the work, we do not find any serious objection. If any do so object, we give Dr. Kennedy's defence of lay agency in the case of 'the Men,' even though it closes with an attack upon our Lowland evangelists:—

'Of the question, "How far lay agency may be employed for the edification of the Church," the wisest practical solution has been furnished in the service of the fellowship meeting. It is surely desirable that, if there are talented and godly men in a congregation, an opportunity should be afforded for securing to others the benefit of those gifts with which the Lord has endowed them. If He has made them "apt to teach," an opportunity to teach should be given them by the Church. This should be provided so as not to invade the province of the ordained teacher, and so as to conserve and support the authority of his office. By no summary process ought a man to be converted into a preacher, however shining his gifts, and however eminent his godliness. But is he therefore to be kept silent? May no opportunity be given him to exhort his brethren, publicly as well as privately, so as to secure to the Church at large the benefit of his stores of Christian knowledge and experience? All these conditions have been met in the service of the fellowship meeting. There an opportunity to exercise their gifts for the good of the Church, and without the least prejudice to the position and influence of the minister, was given to such as the Lord had qualified. How strange it is, that some, who neglect to avail themselves of such an arrangement, and who are disposed to frown upon it where it has been adopted, should not hesitate to exalt into the position even of evangelists, neophytes, with crude views of the doctrines of the gospel, owning subjection to no ecclesiastical authority, and furnishing no security whatever for the prudence and the purity of their doctrine and their life!' (pp. 91, 92).

As to the *thrusting forward* of such laymen (as has been charged against us), we would again cite Dr Kennedy's defence of 'the Men':*—

---

* The peculiar dress of 'the Men,' their long hair and their cloaks, etc., are cer-

'When a godly Highland minister discerned a promise of use-fulness in a man who seemed to have been truly converted unto God, he brought him gradually forward into a more public po-sition, by calling him first to pray, and then "to speak to the ques-tion," at the ordinary congregational meetings. According to the manner in which he approved himself there was the prospect of his being enrolled among "the Friday speakers" on communion occasions. It was thus the order of "the Men" was established, and thus the body of "the Men" was formed.

'The only peculiarity about them, besides their godliness, was their service in the fellowship meeting. This has, to some eyes, the wild look of a great irregularity. It is thought that "the Men" were pushed forward into the position of public speakers by the current of popular feeling, and that the ministers were compelled to share with them their own place in order to reserve any part of it to themselves. Than this there cannot be a greater mis-take' (pp. 87, 88).

'The means taken by men anxious to secure a certain result, and determined to produce it,' are exemplified thus:—

' "Go to the street," said the great American evangelist to a group of young ladies who were seated before him, "and lay your hand on the shoulder of every drunkard you meet, and tell him that God loves him, and that Christ died for him; and *if you do so, I see no reason why there should be an unconverted drunk-ard in Edinburgh for forty-eight hours" '* (p. 21).

Suppose I question the accuracy of this statement, *will Dr. Kennedy name his authority?* No one of us who were daily in the habit of hear-ing Mr. Moody ever heard such a statement from him. But in addi-tion to this, Mr. Moody himself thus writes: 'It *is a false statement;* I do not think it would be a proper thing for a young lady to do, and *I*

---

tainly not defensible. Had any of our 'men' in Edinburgh assumed an outlandish garb and let their locks flow, the outcry would have been great. What would have been wrong in Mid-Lothian cannot be right in Ross-shire. 'The Men' were, we doubt not, good men, but their garb, their wild locks, their manners, were such as to repel. In our Lowland movements we have had no such eccentricities. Were any approach to such peculiarities to show itself, it would be condemned, not de-fended.

never advised it. I spoke of drunkards being treated with kindness, and being told of God's love, but not by young ladies going to them and laying their hands on their shoulder.' Mr. Moody spoke of *Christians in general* going out among these drunkards, and said that if each Christian man and woman were to do their duty thus, all would be thus reached and brought under Christian influence within 48 hours. *He did not say converted.* I was present at nine-tenths of the meetings held in the Assembly Hall, and I never heard anything approaching to it. Suppose I were admitting it; may I not ask Dr. Kennedy to defend it, seeing he has related with approbation the incident of good Mr. Sage employing 'Big Rory' to drag people into church by main force, and stationing the said Rory at the door *with his cudgel* to keep them in? The whole scene is worth quoting:—

'The first man in Lochcarron, in those days, was the champion at the athletic games. Conscious of his strength, and knowing that he would make himself respected by all if he could only lay Big Rory on his back, who was acknowledged to be the strongest man in the district, the minister joined the people on the earliest opportunity at their games. Challenging the whole field, he competed for the prize in putting the stone, tossing the caber, and wrestling, and won an easy victory. His fame was established at once. The minister was now the champion of the district, and none was more ready to defer to him than he whom he had deprived of the laurel. Taking Rory aside to a confidential crack, he said to him: "Now, Rory, I am the minister, and you must be my elder, and we both must see to it that all the people attend church, observe the Sabbath, and conduct themselves properly." Rory fell in with the proposal at once. On Sabbath, when the people would gather to their games in the forenoon, the minister and his elder would join them, and each taking a couple by the hand, they would drag them to the church, lock them in, and then return to catch some more. This was repeated till none was left on the field. Then, stationing the elder with his cudgel at the door, the minister would mount the pulpit and conduct the service' (pp. 59, 60).

It was hardly worth Dr. Kennedy's while to speak as he has done of the young ladies of Edinburgh laying hold of the drunkards, and yet to record with such delight the story of the minister's wrestling, laying Big Rory on his back, tossing the caber, dragging the people in, and setting the elder with his *cudgel* to watch! That which is peculiar in the South may have some counterpart in the North. The cudgel was a terrible thing for a minister or an elder to use for bringing men to the gospel. It looked sadly like trusting in an arm of flesh and ignoring the sovereignty of God. Was Big Rory with his cudgel right, and would the young ladies with their hands have been wrong? The concluding sentence, if ever spoken by any one, could only have been uttered as expressive of the influence of Christian effort in bringing souls to Christ. Suppose some one did actually use the words? He spoke unadvisedly with his lips, as some of us in the South may have done. Possibly some in the North have occasionally done the same.

Dr. Kennedy is jealous, and rightly so, of the good name of his countrymen in the North. He repels with indignation the charge of 'Closetism':—

'Under the vague charge, to which the name of Closetism has been given,—just because it was never distinctly designated before, and because it can only be appropriately when vaguely named,—there are hid insinuations of licentiousness and indolence. It is suspected by some that the religion of the Highlands is something which its possessors never bring out of their closets but to pit it against the religion of others. There never was a fouler calumny than this' (p. 127).

He does not then need to wonder that we also should be jealous of our good men's good names, and that we also repel the charges brought against them and the work which they have done. If we had said the tenth part against the North that he has said against the South, we could comprehend the intensity of his pamphlet, even though we might dispute its justice.

Dr. Kennedy compares the movement to the spasms of a dying child. We prefer to liken it to the throes of a living mother, giving birth to a noble son.

I should like the reader to remember that the greater part of this movement has been carried on not by our American brethren, but by Scottish ministers and elders. In Edinburgh, for instance, the Americans were only present in December and January. After that the work there passed entirely into Scottish hands. The objections that might apply to Mr. Moody cannot apply to the acknowledged ministers of the different churches in our land. It does not follow, that because it might be right to stand aloof from the first part of the work, when it was under what some would call suspicious guidance, that it is equally proper to keep apart from it afterwards, when well-known brethren were conducting it.

Perhaps the most terrible words of this pamphlet are reserved for the last. They are the words of one who has taken up his pen to write words of judgment against his brethren, and who does not seem to entertain any idea of the possibility of his sentence being questioned or set aside by any court of appeal. The words I refer to are the following:— 'spasmodic,'—'convulsions,'—'revivals got up by men,'—'the men who luxuriate in the excitement of man-made revivals,'—'one-sided views of truth,'—'germs of serious errors,'—'lack of spiritual discernment,'—'superficial experience,'—'Arminianism,'—'Plymouthism,'—'galvanising,'—'sensational shocks,'—'temporary bustle,'—'negative theology,'—'unscriptural inventions,'—'the tinsel of a superficial religiousness' (pp. 35,36). Surely the vocabulary has been exhausted. We can hardly conceive of anything worse.

All this is said by *one* brother against hundreds of brethren! The Judge who knoweth all hearts will not thus deal with us, who, it may be, in the midst of much imperfection, have tried to be faithful to our trust.

The judgment here passed upon us is rather too intolerant to commend itself to dispassionate onlookers. It needlessly repels, by taking the worst view of men and things, when censures less one-sided and words less discourteous might have secured at least a patient hearing. The writer has not done justice either to himself or his cause. He has struck too keenly and too rashly. He might have hit some blots, and, with less indiscriminate condemnation, might have at least prevented the recoil which his sharp words must produce. But he has invaded territory on which only Omniscience can set its foot. He has judged the heart. He has let down his fathom-line into depths which only one plummet can sound. He need not wonder should he fail to secure a verdict against us. He has said too much, and he has not said it well. No word of love to brethren breathes through these pages. The Master pities when *He* searches, but the servant searches without one pitying word. O Master, good and kind; rather than this cold scrutiny let us have Thy searching eyes, Thy searching touch, Thy searching breath! From *Thee* we yet may hope for a reversal of this sentence, and for words of compensation which *Thou* only canst utter;—'Well done, good and faithful servant.'

I can hardly admit that, even were the work an unreality, Dr. Kennedy's position and language would be justified. But on the other hand, WHAT IF THAT WORK BE TRUE? What if all his hard words have been spoken against men who have been really doing God's work, and against a work which, with all its imperfections, is essentially divine? He accepts the responsibility of opposing it; I accept the responsibility of upholding it. I cannot but think that the first of these is by far the heavier of the two. To be contending for God, even under a mistake, is not so serious as contending against Him, even though this last hostility may plead the best of motives,—zeal for the honour of Him whose doings in the land are the subject of question. Gamaliel's position would be safer so long as there is the shadow of a doubt as to the matter. 'Refrain from these men, and let them alone; for if this counsel and *this work* be of men, it will come to nought. But if it be of God, ye cannot overthrow it, lest haply ye be found even to fight against God.'

NOTES.

I.—THE GOSPEL.

IN connection with the gospel, I give the two following extracts. The first is from the tract * of Mr. Moore, an Irish Presbyterian minister. I quote it to show the reader the way in which some state the gospel by exhorting the anxious to 'wait at the pool.' I do not here discuss the subject; I merely quote the passage:—

'The natural man can believe in Jesus, but not with a living, spiritual faith. God righteously demands this faith, and the apostles rightly enjoin it, though the natural man can no more believe with this faith than he can leap over the moon....What, then, is a poor, helpless sinner to do? *Do what you can,* and God may enable you to do what you ought, and as He requires. You already believe as you can, and repent as you can, and pray as you can. Go on in this course,—*your only one,*—and who can tell but Jesus will grant His Spirit—nay, has He not promised it?—to transform your dead faith into a living faith, etc.?...Thou hast commanded, "Occupy till I come." Thou hast promised, "To him that hath (improved his talent) shall be given" (more); and Thou hast commended the diligent, "She hath done what she could,"—an angel could do no more. O my soul! what talent, what ability, hath the generous Jesus given thee, *unrenewed though thou art!* To quit the company of godless companions; to go no more to the gambler's table, the drunkard's haunt, the harlot's home; to keep my tongue from blasphemy and lies, my hand from violence and theft; to read, to search God's gospel record; to go with the people of God to the house of God, to hear God's message of mercy; to join, however imperfectly, in divine worship, in prayer, in praise; and to wait and cry, and lie at the pool of Bethesda, till God send His angel to move the waters for thy cure. If I use the rational talents which God has given me, will He not for Christ's sake give me the spiritual talents I require ? (Matt. 25)'

---

* From a tract called *The Plymouth's Prayer Puzzle.*

In opposition to this I quote the following passage from Andrew Fuller, whose uncompromising Calvinism is well known:—

It is the duty of ministers not only to exhort their carnal hearers to believe in Jesus Christ for the salvation of their souls; but IT IS AT OUR PERIL TO EXHORT THEM TO ANYTHING SHORT OF IT, OR WHICH DOES NOT INVOLVE OR IMPLY IT. We have sunk into such a compromising way of dealing with the unconverted as to have well-nigh lost sight of the spirit of the primitive preachers; and hence it is that sinners of every description can sit so quietly as they do in our places of worship. Christ and His apostles, without any hesitation, called on sinners to repent and believe the gospel; but we, considering them as poor, impotent, and depraved creatures, have been disposed to drop this part of the Christian ministry. Considering such things as beyond the power of their hearers, they seem to have contented themselves with pressing on them the things they *could* perform, still continuing enemies of Christ—such as behaving decently in society, reading the Scriptures, and attending the means of grace. Thus it is that hearers of this description sit at ease in our congregations. But as this implies no *guilt* on their part, they sit unconcerned, conceiving that all that is required of them is to lie in the way and wait the Lord's time. But is this the religion of the Scriptures? Where does it appear that the prophets or apostles treated that kind of inability which is merely the effect of reigning aversion as affording any excuse? And where have they descended in their exhortations to things which might be done, and the parties still continue the enemies of God? Instead of leaving out everything of a spiritual nature because their hearers could not find it in their hearts to comply with it, it may be safely affirmed that they exhorted to nothing else, treating such inability not only as of no account with regard to the lessening of obligation, but as rendering the subjects of it worthy of the severest rebuke....Repentance toward God, and faith towards our Lord Jesus Christ, are allowed to be duties, but not *immediate* duties. The sinner is considered as unable to comply with them, and therefore they are not urged upon him; but instead of them he is directed to pray for the Holy Spirit to enable him to repent and believe. This, it seems, he *can* do, notwithstanding the aversion of his heart from everything of the kind! But if any man be required to pray for the Holy Spirit, it must be either sincerely and in the name of Jesus, or insincerely and in some other way. The latter, I suppose, will be allowed to be an abomination in the sight of God; he cannot, therefore, be required to do this. And as to the former, it is just as difficult and as opposite to the carnal heart as repentance and faith themselves. Indeed, it amounts to the same thing; for *a sincere desire after a spiritual blessing, presented in the name of Jesus, is no other than the prayer of faith'* (pp. 101-103).

II.—TESTIMONIES TO MR. MOODY.

Injurious statements, founded on a letter from Chicago (the name of the writer of which was withheld), were circulated in various quarters. The author of the letter was evidently no credible nor competent witness, yet its statements were set against the testimony of Scottish brethren. Letters from brethren of all denominations in America immediately afterwards came pouring in upon us, denying the truth of the charges. Take the two following specimens of the counter testimony. The first is a letter to a friend from the well-known Mr. Kimball of Boston,—a man who for some thirty or forty years has had the ear and the confidence of the American Churches as a Christian and as an author:—

'I know Mr. Moody intimately,' Mr. Kimball writes. 'He was converted in our church. The first dawn of his intellect Godward revealed itself in that question to a clerk of mine who was teaching him about Moses, "Well, now, I suppose that Moses was what we call a smart man?" Out of the rough of ignorance God has wrought a man in a million. He is one of the best, truest, most useful, and devoted that I know.'—(Boston, December 30, 1873.)

Mr. T. De Witt Talmage, of Brooklyn, thus writes to myself, May 23, 1874:—

'DEAR BROTHER,—We congratulate you all on what God is doing in Scotland through the instrumentality of D. L. Moody. You cannot cherish him too highly. We who have known him intimately believe in him through and through. He has the full confidence of all our Churches. I shall never forget the sermon he preached in my pulpit at the Brooklyn Tabernacle. Wherever he has gone in our country the divine blessing has gone with him. He does not belong to Chicago, but to the whole Christian Church.'

We have had many similar and most satisfactory testimonies, completely refuting the charges brought against him in the letter from Chicago. But it is impossible to give these in full. I append to this pamphlet the certificate of upwards of thirty ministers of various denominations in Chicago. It is very honourable to Mr. Moody. From it the reader will see how completely we were justified in receiving Mr. Moody not only as a brother in the Lord, but as a 'fellow-worker unto the kingdom of God.'

Chicago, *May 21st,* 1874.

WE, the undersigned Pastors of the City of Chicago, learning that the Christian character of D. L. MOODY has been attacked, for the purpose of destroying his influence as an Evangelist in Scotland, hereby certify that his labours in the Young Men's Christian Association, and as an Evangelist in this City and elsewhere, according to the best information we can get, have been Evangelical and Christian in the highest sense of those terms; and we do not hesitate to commend him as an earnest Christian worker, worthy of the confidence of our Scotch and English brethren, with whom he is now labouring; believing that the Master will be honoured by them in so receiving him among them as a *co-labourer* in the vineyard of the Lord.

> A. J. JUTKINS,
> > Presiding Elder of Chicago Dist.
> C. H. FOWLER,
> > President North-Western University.
> ARTHUR EDWARDS,
> > Editor North-Western Christian Advocate
> > (Methodist Organ), Chicago.
> M. C. BRIGGS.
> S. M'CHESNER,
> > Pastor of the Trinity M. E. Church.
> W. H. DANIELS,
> > Pastor Park Ave. M. E. Church, Chicago.
> SANFORD WASHBURN,
> > Pastor Holsted St. Chur., Methodist Episc.
> C. S. SAMUELL
> > Genl. Supt. Chicago Relief and Aid Society,
> > and Pastor Stock Yards Mission.

WM. F. STEWART,
    Sec. Preachers' Aid Society.
G. S. S. STUFF,
    Pastor Fulton St. M. E. Church.
T. P. MARSH,
    Pastor Austin M. E. Church.
LEWIS MEREDITH,
    Pastor Oakland M. E. Church.
ARTHUR MITCHELL,
    Pastor First Presb. Ch.
GLEN WOOD,
    Western Sec. American Tract Society.
C. D. HELMER,
    Pastor Union Park Congregational Church.
ARTHUR SWAYZEY,
    Pastor Ashland Av. Presbyterian Church.
Rev. N. F. RAVLIN
    Pastor Temple Ch.
A. G. EBENHART,
    Ass. Pastor.
DAVID J. BURREL,
    Pastor Westminster Presbyterian Church.
DAVID SWING,
    Fourth Pres. Church.
L. T. CHAMBERLAIN,
    Pastor of New England Congl. Church.
EDWARD F. WILLIAMS, }
EDWARD N. PACKARD, }
JOHN KIMBALL,   }
W. A. LLOYD,   }
C. A. SOWLE,   }   Congregational
JOHN BRADSHAW,   }   Ministers.
C. F. REED,   }
S. F. DICKINSON,   }
A. WESLEY BILL,   }
ALBERT BUSHNELL, }
EDWARD P. GOODWIN, }
T.W. GOODIFORD.
W. A. BARTLETT.
R. W. PATTERSON.
W. W. EVERTS.

Pastors Of 1st }
    Cong. Ch.   }
2d Baptist.
Plymouth Cong. Ch.
2d Pres. Ch.
1st Baptist.

STATE OF ILLINOIS, COOK COUNTY SS.,
CITY OF CHICAGO.

W. W. VANARSDALE, being first duly sworn upon oath, says that he is the Superintendent of the Young Men's Christian Association of the city of Chicago, Illinois, and that he knows the foregoing signatures to be genuine.

W.W. VANARSDALE

Subscribed and sworn to before me, this 26th day of May A.D. 1874.

ISAAC H. PEDRICK,
Notary Public.

Part Three:

A REPLY

JOHN KENNEDY

A REPLY

TO

DR. BONAR'S

DEFENCE OF HYPER-EVANGELISM.

BY

J. KENNEDY, D.D.
DINGWALL.

"Watch ye, stand fast in the faith, quit you like men, be strong. Let all
your things be done with charity."—1 COR. xvi. 13,14.

EDINBURGH:
LYON & GEMMELL,
15 GEORGE IV. BRIDGE.
1875.

PRICE SIXPENCE.

"Christianity" "does not fear to speak the stern word of condemnation against error."..."Let us not misjudge strong words in controversy.
The religion of both Old and New Testament is marked by fervent, out-
spoken testimonies against evil. To speak smooth things in such a case
may be sentimentalism, but it is not Christianity."..."I know that charity covereth a multitude of sins, but it does not call evil good, because
a good man has done it; it does not excuse inconsistencies because the
inconsistent brother has a high name and a fervent spirit"—*God's Way
of Holiness,* by Dr. H. Bonar, p. 201.

A REPLY, &c.

MY pamphlet, regarding, "The Recent Religious Movement in Scotland," I wrote because I felt constrained to do so. I had formed, with great care, an opinion as to the character of that movement. My estimate was decidedly unfavourable. Because it was so I felt bound to re-examine the grounds on which I had based it. I knew, too, that my conclusions differed from those of many fathers and brethren, whom I regarded with affection and respect. While the movement was confined to the South, there were others, more loudly called than I, to sound a note of warning. But at last the movement came to my door. I was constrained to act a part bearing upon it. The urgent zeal of its promoters compelled me, either to join in it, or to give my reasons for avoiding it. I was thus driven to speak out. I knew what a strong current I had to oppose; and my heart sometimes quivered with the craven fear of the consequences of setting myself against it. This fear I saw to be that which "bringeth a snare;" and I shrunk from it. The fear of yielding to a fear urged me to say my say decidedly. Could I have forgotten the feeling that had almost silenced me, I might have taken more pains to be soft. But thunders of applause were filling the air all around me. The most extravagant statements of results were published in periodicals, specially started to record the running story of the movement, and in all the newspapers, with but few exceptions. To be heard at all, on the other side, one must "lift his voice like a trumpet." Let it sound harshly if it may, it must at least be loud. I thus felt constrained to write, and to do so decidedly. I feared to take pains to be gentle; I was careful only to be distinct.

I did not, nor do I now, think, that my not taking part in the movement disqualified me for forming an opinion regarding it. I am much more disposed to think, that it was just on that account I was competent fairly to judge. "He has looked on it from the outside, not from the inside," is Dr. Bonar's account of my standpoint. So far, he is right; but he ceases to be so when he adds, "afar off, not near." *I was near enough to be able to look into the inside.* If, standing outside, I had in my heart an earnest desire to find that the most sanguine estimate of the work was also the truest, and was straining a wistful eye to discover what would assure me that it was, I occupied a more favourable position, for forming an opinion, than if, still hesitating, I had gone into it, to be swayed by the force of the current into which I had entered. In such a case, finding myself hastily committed, I would be very apt to shut my eyes to all that would seem to make doubtful the propriety of my conduct. In order to justify myself, I would have to accredit the movement, and all chance of impartiality would be gone. Expressions of unqualified approval may, in some instances, thus be accounted for.

I care not to complain of the *tone* of Dr. Bonar's reply. I cannot profess to like it; but I am quite disposed to excuse it. He began to write under the impression that I had started up as an agent of "the accuser of the brethren," to hurl firebrands at his head, and at those of hundreds of his friends. He came thus greatly excited to his task, full of indignation which he regarded as righteous, and quite disposed to think, that any shafts, aimed at me, if only hurled with a strong hand, would pass through me to the enemy of all truth and righteousness. I cannot therefore wonder at the tone of his reply. I rather wonder that, having of me the impression which he formed, he did not still more sharpen and multiply his arrows. A good man cannot be calm when "the accuser of the brethren" is before him. I wonder, too, that one so resolute to strike me should yet call me brother.

But did I really put myself into the association in which Dr. Bonar thinks I am involved? "In Dr. Kennedy's pamphlet, from the title to the last page, no name occurs save his own," is Dr. Bonar's own testimony. So far then, I was not personal in my remarks. I carefully limited the area of the teaching which I condemned, and Dr. Bonar and his "two or three hundred brethren" were not within the lines which I drew. To this further extent I was not personal, at least so far as he and they were concerned. I had absolutely nothing to do with individuals, except in so far as they homologated the views and practices to which I referred. For that involvement, where it exists, I am not responsible. Could I have executed the work to which I set myself and more carefully avoided all offensive references to individuals? If I at all thought of him and of his brethren, it was only when I wrote, "it grieves one's heart to know that this is tolerated, and even approved of, by some who ought to be more zealous for the grace and glory of the Lord, than to be able to endure it." I may have thought of Dr. Bonar when I penned these words; as I think of him now they fitly express my feeling, and they do so, just in the measure in which I still respect and love him.

Dr. Bonar is utterly mistaken in thinking that I was aiming at "the current theology," and bringing charges "against brethren of all churches." I was aiming at no theology but that which I described. If that were "the current theology," then I did attack it, but not otherwise. But that is not "the current theology" yet, though Dr. Bonar and his friends are unconsciously doing what they can to make it so. My pamphlet was directed against no brethren of any of all the churches. If Dr. Bonar and his brethren stand up before that, at which alone I aimed, they must not lay to my account what they owe only to themselves. Fain would I that they were far away from the line of my fire. But to Mr. Bonar I am as Haman, who "thought scorn to lay hands on Mordecai alone, wherefore he sought to destroy all the Jews that were throughout the whole kingdom, even the people of Mordecai." I cannot therefore wonder that he dipped his pen in gall, and tipped with fire his arrows. And instead of being disposed to whine over my being described as one vindictive as Haman, and more unfair than Newman, as Dr. Bonar describes me, I take help from these aspersions in condoning much besides which his pamphlet contains. Of one answering this description he could not but write hard things. But as such was I before his mind, and as an honest man he could not but try to write me down.

I am quite persuaded that many, who took an active part in the movement, had previously no sympathy with the kind of teaching which I assailed, and, if it lacked the recommendation of seeming success, would not tolerate it even now. But there is a strong tendency, on the part of the soundest, to glide into what they see to be effective, and, owing to their sanguine estimate of its results, to adopt it as their own. To them the new element in the doctrine seems to be what accounts for the fruit. The greater power is ascribed to that which was awanting in their own previous teaching, and they mingle the novelty with "the old gospel" in order to increase their usefulness. Of this tendency Dr. Bonar's pamphlet affords sufficient evidence.

I am quite ready to allow that, in the addresses of those who hold the views to which I refer, there will be found statements that seem to contradict those which are objectionable. This, however, does not prove that the bearing of the teaching, as a whole, is not what I indicated. The telling part of the doctrine may be that which is unscriptural, and all the more is it helped to be so by the mixture of what tends to recommend it to acceptance. The measure of truth it contains merely serves, in many cases, to throw conscience off its guard. It seems to some, as if the utterance of an occasional statement, that is both indefensible and dangerous, can be quite counteracted by other statements, from the same source, that are confessedly scriptural. But in such a case, the character and tendency of the teaching are not determined by the counterpoise of truth. The sound doctrine cannot be intelligently apprehended and honestly believed, if what is utterly inconsistent with it is both held and proclaimed. A breach in the wrapping exposes the contents of a parcel. To that opening the eye must be directed that would discover what the envelope enclosed. An occasional erroneous statement, breaking wildly through the bounds of possible orthodoxy, exposes the spirit of one's teaching, and is the index of its practical tendency.

I am not to complain of the *mode* of Dr. Bonar's reply. Regarding me as an enemy to what, in his view, is a great work of God, he deemed it quite legitimate to attempt to weaken my testimony by damaging myself. If he could only prove me incompetent and prejudiced, he would succeed in weaning all respect from my opinion. To this work he therefore sets himself. And he does it "with a will." Of this I care not to complain. He chose his way and has to render his account. I might take exception to the state of feeling which led him to misjudge me; but forming of me the estimate, which he allowed himself to form, he felt justified in doing what he could to expose me. I believe that in the hardest things, which he said against me, he was conscious only of a feeling which he regarded as but weakly righteous. Instead, therefore, of being provoked to resentment, I would rather thank him for the kindly memories which preserved him from a still harsher utterance.

The lack of calmness, system, and logic in "the old gospel," I ascribe entirely to undue excitement, produced by the harsh judgment which he formed of my spirit and intention. I regret both the harsh judgement and its effects; but not because Dr. Bonar's reply has in the very least degree disturbed my conscience. I regret the former, because I would fain have another place, in a brother's regard, than that which he accords; and I regret the latter, because of the difficulty I find in arranging the contents of his pamphlet, so as to have them systematically before me. I can quite recall my intention as I was writing; and though then, as always, there was much that was amiss in my state of feeling, there was not mingled with it any disposition to set myself above, nor to censure, any of all my brethren. Dr. Bonar thinks he found, in the first page of my pamphlet, evidence of most offensive assumption, in the words, "Sad, yea, strained to breaking, must be the heart of one, who seeks the glory of God and the salvation of souls, if he cannot share in the prevalent hopefulness and joy." I never intended to represent myself as such a one. I felt inclined rather to be ashamed that I was not so affected. But what I could say, without fear of uttering a falsehood, I did say of myself, when I added the words which follow, in which I represent myself as "one of those to whom the present movement has hitherto yielded more grief than gladness."

Dr. Bonar insists that, in forming and publishing an opinion of the movement, I committed the very mistake which I imputed to those who, at the outset, proclaimed it to be a work of God; and there is a rather amusing attempt to be logical in a footnote bearing upon this. I did say, and I now repeat, that "it may be legitimate to form an *unfavourable* opinion, even at the outset, of a religious awakening, *if the means employed in producing it are such as the Lord cannot be expected to bless.*" Does Dr. Bonar really intend to deny this? And is it not true that fruit-bearing is the only evidence of genuine discipleship? If so, how, ere the fruit is produced, can a *favourable* judgment be confidently announced? Is there any other way in which believers can make their calling and election sure, but that which is indicated in 2 Pet. 1:1-10? What, then, means the laboured footnote, which, if it had been assigned to its proper place, would have been left for the page after the last of the pamphlet?

Dr. Bonar attempts to damage my testimony—1. By alleging that I have an anti-revival prejudice. 2. By insisting that I had not sufficient evidence. And 3. By ascribing to me a blinding anti-lowland feeling.

1. DR. BONAR ALLEGES THAT I AM PREJUDICED AGAINST REVIVALS

HE quotes, from my memoir of my father, a passage describing his state of feeling in reference to the revival that spread over Ross-shire, as well as other parts of the country, shortly before his death in 1841, which he offers as a proof of my having always had a prejudice against such movements. Why my father's feeling should be mine he does not tell. But I can assure him that, whatever my opinion of such movements in recent times has been, it is mine, not because I inherited it, but as the result of an experience all my own.

To a fear of a religious movement being misjudged I confess. I also confess to a tendency not to be very sanguine as to results. But I cannot help this. My experience has been such as necessarily to induce that state of feeling.

I early found myself in the midst of a revival movement. It was in the Highlands, too. The preaching which was mainly instrumental in producing it was preaching which I greatly admired. "The Apostle of the North" was the leader then. Hundreds have I seen deeply affected in one congregation. This was the season, too, when the crisis of my own life had come. I went then to hear the gospel as one to whom the issue was to be life or death for ever. I craved with all my heart to share in the impression made on other hearts, if it verily resulted from the operation of the Spirit's power. But the greater the excitement, the less, to my consciousness, the power. I well remember when, in the midst of hundreds of mourners, an old man, who had spent the two nights preceding on the hill-side in an agony of distress, arose, and, in a loud wail, exclaimed, *"tha mi caillte"* (I am lost). But not four days had passed before he was as callous and as worldly as before. Nor was his case, in its last phase, an exceptional one; for those who knew the district well could tell of scarce any abiding fruit as the result of that remarkable movement.

From this experience in the Highlands I passed to Aberdeen, and found myself there in the midst of the movement, in which William Burns was the leader. For that man of God, with his rare talents, his rich attainments, his devotional spirit, and his burning zeal, those who knew him had such respect, as if in him an apostle of Jesus Christ had risen again from the dead. I was a witness to the marvellous effects of his addresses. I went to hear him with a fervent desire to be impressed; but, with all my reverence for the preacher, and my heart's hunger for benefit from his services, I was constrained even then, young and inexperienced as I was, to conclude that his method was not judicious. Five or six addresses he would sometimes deliver during the time of service, assured that what he said was given to him, and that when he ceased to speak, it was because the Lord had ceased to supply. This impressed me, even then, as indicating far more zeal than discretion, and as what would, in the case of a less gifted and spiritual man, be very dangerous. A year thereafter, I was present when Mr. Burns asked those who were impressed, during his former visit, to meet in a certain place at an appointed hour. I resolved to be, and I was, present there and then. Eleven young women appeared, and no more; and their cases, if one might judge by their demeanour, were not very hopeful. I am far from saying that this was all the fruit of the wonderful movement in Aberdeen; and, even after this experience, my soul was fired with indignation at the conduct of the men who scoffingly decried it, and would brand the servant of the Lord, because of his earnestness in seeking to bring souls to Christ. Precious would the fruit have been, if but these eleven had been truly turned to God, for unspeakably great is the salvation of one soul. But how different this result from the sanguine estimate of the year before, when Mr. Burns, as he pointed to hundreds before him, declared his persuasion that they were all true converts! Mr. Burns entered the place of meeting, looked down on the little group before him, crossed his arms on the book-board, bent his head on them, and wept. That most impressive scene I cannot forget. I learned a life-lesson then. But, as surely as I saw this, do I expect that some of those dear brethren, whose hopes are now so high, shall, erewhile, have a like sorrow to endure.

Soon after I became a preacher, I was in a district, where such was the people's sensitiveness of feeling, that I could not read the opening psalm without many being in tears, and the sounds of sobbing compelling me to pause. A sensational address would have laid the whole congregation prostrate on the earth. But this impression passed like a morning cloud away.

I went to Ireland during the great revival season. I went panting to find the best accounts that I had heard to be true. So ardently did I seek this, that I scarce think I could have endured the joy of not being disappointed. I had ample opportunity of examining the first results of the movement. I was present at a converts' meeting. There was a desk for preaching practice at one side of the hall in which they were assembled. One after another mounted it, and delivered a discourse. I heard four of these, but in none of them was there any reference to the law, to the necessity of regeneration, to the Divine person or atoning blood of Christ, or to any of the Divine perfections but love. Vague declamation about the danger of unbelief, and the desirableness of peace and joy in believing, was all that they contained. I thought then, and I still think, that the themes ignored by those speakers could not be passed over in a true convert's address; and I was not unprepared for the answer given, two years thereafter, by an Irish minister, to my question, when I asked, "What is now the result of the revival in your district?" His reply was, "During that wonderful movement I laboured with all my strength, and at such a pitch of hope, that I thought none around me would remain unsaved; but, at this moment, I know no result besides the spread of Plymouthism, and a prevalent contempt for the stated means of grace, the last of those whom I regarded as converts having recently gone back to the world."

These experiences have so affected me, that I cannot be sanguine as to the results of such a movement as lately pervaded our land. If I was so disappointed when the doctrine and mode of service were scriptural, I must not, by a hasty hopefulness, prepare for a sorer disappointment in connection with a movement in which these accord not with the Word of God.

Why will Dr. Bonar and others fear only the danger of not countenancing what is a work of God? Is there no danger on the other side? Their one fear tends to make them tolerant of all that accompanies what they regard as a work of grace. All modes of teaching, and all forms of worship, that have around them the halo of what is deemed a blessing from on high, are apt to be regarded as divinely sanctioned, and, as such, to receive unquestioning acceptance. How much may thus be introduced by an enemy's hand, to be a standing hindrance to the progress of truth and godliness! And if the work prove not to be what was expected, how disastrous its effect must be! I have seen so much of this, that I cannot but fear it. Where I expected a "wilderness" to be changed into a "garden of the soul," I have only seen a desert becoming more a waste than before.

Looking over the known results of revival movements in our country, I have the impression that, in connection with each of them, there was, to a greater or less extent, a genuine work of grace, but that this was not unfrequently covered out of sight by a superficial excitement, which alone caught the eye of the public. In their efforts to increase this latter, men were unconsciously working out a design of the enemy, who would fain implicate in it the honour of vital godliness, that he might, by proved failures, bring discredit on the Spirit's work, and thus confirm the unbelief, and deepen the sleep, of worldlings. And I am persuaded that the teacher would act a more Christ-like part who, in such circumstances, brought searching doctrine to bear on the impressed. This would save the cause of true religion from being so much involved in cases which can only be occasions of reproach. The first results might not bulk so largely, but the abiding fruit would be a more unmingled blessing. It was thus that Jesus dealt with an excited crowd, though the result was that "many of his disciples went back, and walked no more with him."

2. DR. BONAR INSISTS THAT I LACKED SUFFICIENT EVIDENCE

He makes, repeats, and reiterates a demand for evidence in support of charges brought against him and his brethren. Not having preferred such charges, no *onus probandi*, in reference to them, lies on my shoulders. If he asked for proof of the dangerous influence of the teaching to which I referred, he himself would have met his demand with supply; for there is far too much evidence of this in his pamphlet. How I wish it were less; and that, standing out clear from all that I condemned, he had allowed me to be quite as sure as I had previously been, that he certainly adhered to "such a system as the Shorter Catechism contains."

He insists that, in the face of ample evidence in favour of the work, I have indiscriminately censured both it and its promoters. He contrasts my state of feeling with the charity and gladness of the Church at Jerusalem during the first great revival of New Testament times. "No word of hope is spoken by him," he says. This is not the fact; but he was so occupied with what annoyed him, that my words of hope were quite unnoticed. But it was only by ignoring these that he could manage the contrast which he was anxious to draw. And did the Church at Jerusalem receive the first tidings of a revival with unquestioning gladness? No; but they sent Barnabas to visit the scene of the work. He went, and saw what, with his gift of discernment, he regarded as a genuine work of grace. This gladdened him; and, being known to be "a good man, and full of the Holy Ghost and of faith," his report of the work would, doubtless, give joy to the brethren who sent him. Without such a report, by such a man, the Church at Jerusalem would not be satisfied, for they refused to receive Paul himself as a convert till they first had tried him. The Church, then, if they did not act under infallible guidance, did not act "quickly," and therefore "prematurely," in receiving those who professed to be believers. They did admit converts very early into the Church, through the administration of the appointed sealing ordinance; but they did not tell them, before they admitted them, that they were converts. They left the responsibility of determining that question on themselves. Dr. Bonar misstates both sides of his contrast.

But, while not claiming to be like Barnabas, Dr. Bonar thinks that he and "some hundreds of the servants of the Lord Jesus Christ" may surely weigh as much as one Barnabas, and should be believed as he was by the Church at Jerusalem. Certainly not, if his own account of them be true when he says, "We cannot discern spirits." The testimony of one Barnabas, with that gift, is better than that which "some hundreds" without it can accumulate. Let him not wonder, therefore, that I cannot adopt their conclusion as my own.

I know not what Dr. Bonar means by constantly holding up the balances with "some hundreds" of credible witnesses in the one scale, and the author of "Hyper-Evangelism" all alone in the other. If he were merely balancing weight of character, he might be content to leave out his associates. He himself alone would have sufficed. He added a needless makeweight when he put the others in. When he still holds out the scales before me, I refuse to go myself into the one he appoints for me; but I again throw into it my *statements,* and let him fill the other as he may; I fearlessly await the result. In his attempt to weigh *conclusions,* he holds the balances in a weak and unsteady hand.

The description which I gave of "the more prominent teaching under which the movement has advanced," was not drawn up without care. I cannot think that I required more ample materials, than were before me, for forming an opinion. With the style of teaching I had been familiar long before this last movement began. I had occasion to test it in my youth, when my eternal all was consciously at stake on its soundness; for I had imbibed its views, and had experience of the peace it can give, and of the zeal it can excite. I had studied it in connection with previous movements, which were regarded as revivals. I was anxious to do so, that I might have some idea how these were likely to affect the religious condition of the country. In connection with earlier crusades of occasional "evangelists," I formed an opinion of the doctrine which won their seeming success. I found, too, that organisations were being formed to keep up their kind of teaching. In connection with these, again, I studied the subject. When this last movement began, I came to examine the doctrine of its leader, with the earnest desire to find it quite different from that which I previously regarded as faulty. It was with no other prepossession I began to look into it; and my being constrained to form, was at least as painful as it was formidable to publish, an unfavourable opinion.

It may serve a controversial purpose to represent me as unable, because prejudiced, fairly to use the materials which lay at my hand; but sufficient evidence I had. I am charged with contenting myself with "anonymous hearsay evidence," and with having, therefore, acted less honourably than the moderates of Aberdeen when they examined into the credentials of the revival under William Burns. But there is no ground for any such accusation. In the quotations which I gave, I was careful even to the syllables. Only in one syllable, to which I shall afterwards refer, have I any correction to make. In not the slightest degree have I misrepresented the views of the speaker from whose addresses I quoted. I mentioned no authorities, because I mainly depended on the evidence of my own ears; and the little which I added to what I myself heard is, I know, quite as accurately given. I adduced no witnesses, for I regarded my own right ear and my left as parts of myself, and I rather shrank from the operation required to prepare them for being separately produced.

There is one quotation, which Dr. Bonar questions because he never heard it, and which Mr. Moody declares to be inaccurate, because he cannot recollect it. But it happens to be one which I myself heard, and I know that I have given the very words which were spoken. Dr. Bonar draws attention mainly to the first words of the quotation, to which, though they were spoken, I attached no importance. I did not intend to give the impression that Mr. Moody directed the young ladies to do an indelicate thing, when he told them to put their hand on the shoulder of a drunkard. I never even dreamed of that as an impropriety. But it is to that both the doctor and the evangelist mainly refer. I can conceive why the former did so. It gave him an opportunity of trying to use "big Rory's cudgel" in an assault on me. If the wrestler were alive, and the cudgel in his grasp, I am rather disposed to think that he would not have ventured to do so, especially if "Rory" knew that he was to use his stick against a Highlander. But the attempt to use the cudgel of the dead against his countryman was as foolish as it was cowardly. If I wrote that in the wild days of the Highlands, when he himself was the wildest of the wild, an athlete had used his stick in driving people to the house of God, what bearing has this on the question, whether it was right to say that, if the drunkards of Edinburgh were told that God loved them, there was no reason why they should not be all converted? This was the only thing, in the statement quoted, which I deemed of importance, and therefore I gave it in italics. If I had said that "big Rory" had converted men by his cudgel, the use of this against me might have been relevant. And yet, if I had said so, I would have written just as soberly as the man spoke, who said that young ladies could have converted them by telling them what, in any case, would be unwarranted, and in some cases false. But here again I am at issue with the great "evangelist," who, in the hearing of hundreds, said, "Jesus loved Judas Iscariot as surely as he loved Simon

Peter." Will Dr. Bonar deny that this was said? or will he homologate the statement if he knows that it was uttered? I am at issue, too, with him and with those who responded to him when he asked, at the close of a great meeting in Glasgow, "If there was any hindrance to the conversion of all present that night." "None," was the unhesitating reply, given in a firm tone, heard over the whole palace. The same question was put to Dr. Bonar, and then to Mr. Sankey, and the same answer was given.—*Times of Blessing, May* 21, 1874, p. 95.

I call attention to this, because I regard it as giving us the keynote of all the teaching which has proved effective in advancing this movement. "Is there any hindrance?" Yes, there are all the hindrances which the lusts of the flesh, the power of spiritual death, the influence of the world, and the wiles and might of Satan can furnish, to make it impossible that, without the Almighty power of God, any one of them all should be converted. And who was there to presume to tell that God would do it? Had the question assumed the form of asking whether all present had a warrant to believe in Christ, or whether the power of God sufficed for the conversion of them all, it might have been put and responded to in all sobriety and truthfulness. But in the form in which it was put, it indicated a thorough ignoring of the depravity of human nature, and of the sovereignty and power of God. The spirit of the movement burst out in that question, and exposed itself as the very kind of thing which I have represented it to be.

To a footnote on page 47 (p. 77) of Dr. Bonar's pamphlet I must here refer, because it deals with what he calls a specimen of "the serious inaccuracies scattered throughout" my pamphlet. The words to which he refers were undoubtedly spoken by Mr. Moody with one exception. Instead of the word "raise," he used the word "*lug.*" With that correction, I adhere to the quotation as formerly given. As to the quoted counsel, Dr. Bonar says, "Whoever said it spoke unadvisedly with his lips." In this, at any rate, he and I are thoroughly agreed. But he is anxious to excuse it notwithstanding, and he cites Luther, to cover with the shield of his authority the dangerous advice. But Luther refuses the office. He, intent on setting free from legal bondage an anxious soul, addresses "the law of works" as a master from whose yoke the believer is free. Yet in his address to the law, we have a confession of numberless daily sins. How different this from the doctrine that confession of sin is to be dispensed with, and that joy, with no attendant sorrow, is what Christians should seek to attain.

3. DR. BONAR CHARGES ME WITH A BLINDING ANTI-LOWLAND PREJUDICE

"I HAVE another reason," he says, "for not being surprised at Dr. Kennedy's objections to the Southern revival. I find that many of the Ross-shire fathers, who were the leaders in the Northern movement, were men who had what is called the 'second-sight,' and who had the gift of prophecy." "The biographer of these men will naturally look suspiciously upon the men of the South, who have not the peculiarities of the North, and question the depth of any movement going on under them." He then gives a few instances of what he refers to, not because they have any relevant bearing on the question at issue, but because in some minds they might help to excite a prejudice against me.

I knew not, till Dr. Bonar informed me, that they "are not able to produce any such instances of prophetic discernment in the South," as those which he quotes. I only knew that in the days of Dr. Love, there was, at least, one in the South who was not a stranger to these things, and that, in still earlier days, as they of the South themselves do tell us, there were not a few in their region who had very remarkable "prophetic discernment." If I had cared to think about it, I perhaps might, without Dr. Bonar's help, have discovered that they in the South, now-a-days, were not acquainted with these things. But till he himself suggested it, I confess I never made any effort to inquire. I never even thought of himself and his brethren in connection with this "peculiarity." I may sometimes have considered how he and his associates would compare with the men whom the Lord, in other days, gave with His blessing to Ross-shire, as to a clear view, and a firm grasp, of the truth, and as to keenness of discernment for trying "the spirits, whether they be of God;" and, now that he has provoked me to do so again, I have attained to a persuasion that, in these things, they are quite as far behind the Ross-shire fathers, as in that of which it is their boast to be ignorant. But if I cannot say that I expected them to compare favourably with the fathers of Ross-shire, I did expect that their spirit would savour less of the moderatism which once maligned and oppressed them.

Dr. Bonar's only object in giving these quotations from my book, was to form a circuitous connection between the northern peculiarity and the subject of the revival, such as would seem to give him an op-

portunity of exciting a feeling against the author of "Hyper-Evangelism."
It is simply silly to say, that "the existence of these things cannot be
regarded as any proof of the greater depth in the North." No one ever
appealed to them as such; for they never were associated in any way,
or to any extent, with the work of conversion at all.

What he quotes as instances of "prophetic discernment," or "second-sight," as he chooses to call it, is a mere narrative of facts, given
on the authority of men who were never known to lie, or according to
evidence furnished by my senses, with some corroborating testimony
from consciousness. In writing this, I knew that I would expose myself to sneers not a few; but I also knew that, if I did not write it, those
who came after me would not be likely to do so, and that this feature,
be it a defect or the reverse, would be awanting from the portrait left
to the generations to come, of the religion that spread its blessed influence, with unique effect, over the Highlands of Scotland.

In excusing the record of them, I did write that "the improbability
of such things to the minds of *some,* is owing to their own utter estrangement from the Lord." Does Dr. Bonar really think that I intended this to apply to him and to his brethren, or to any like-mind-
ed men? I intended it to apply to those whom I described, and to none
besides. And yet he actually misrepresents me, as having "unadvisedly censured those who, without in the least 'sneering' at them, feel
constrained to ask for fuller evidence."

In accounting for the strange facts which I gave, illustrative of peculiar nearness to God in the case of some ministers in the North, I
did say that they were tokens of the Lord's presence "to a simple and
uneducated people, unable to appreciate the standing evidences of the
gospel," in order to increase His servants' influence. I am charged with
Irvingism for saying this. If I regarded these things as miraculous, I
would be open to such a charge. But Dr. Bonar will find, in the very
book from which he quoted, that I have endeavoured to prove, and, as
I think, successfully, that they were not miraculous at all. And, even
if they were, he who expects such a shower of miracles to usher in the
glory of the latter days, is not the man I would suspect of being scep-
tical as to preclude drops falling even on our times.

I deeply regret to find Dr. Bonar serving himself heir to a calumny of "the men," for which he makes room in a footnote. He speaks of
them as wearing a peculiar garb, and affecting a peculiar manner, and
he contrasts them with the trim laymen of the South. Their poverty
alone left its mark on their attire; this was their only reproach, so far
as their clothing was concerned. To twit them with this is a still greater

reproach. Their manner was peculiar, only because they cared not to adapt it to the fashion of the world, and because it differed from the flippancy of graceless formalists.

"His standard differs from ours. His point of view is not at all the same as ours." This, he alleges, must be the case, because I am in the North, and they in the South. I can scarcely tell whether it is so or not, till I distinctly know what their standard is. What he intends to say is, that in the South they have the right, and that in the North we have the wrong, standard. "I," he says, "can separate what is doubtful from what is certain, what is scriptural from what is not;" "they in the North cannot do so" is implied, though not expressed. I certainly am not disposed to pit my discernment against that of Dr. Bonar, or of any other; but, such as it is, I alone am responsible for the use of it, and cannot, therefore,—not because I count it better than that of others, but because it is mine, and not another's—blindly follow the lead of any men, whether in the South or North. Under a sense of that responsibility, I formed, and, being persuaded that it was right, I published, an opinion regarding the recent religious movement in Scotland. That persuasion has not yet been shaken—it has been rather confirmed,—and Dr. Bonar's "Old Gospel" has only helped to strengthen it. Most honestly may I say, that I had preferred if he had broken down my position, and swept me into the current in which he himself is moving, if I could carry with me into his fellowship the same strength of conviction which still keeps me aloof.

If I must produce my standard, that he may place his beside it, I have to tell him that, in trying a case of seeming conversion, in order to know whether it is likely to prove genuine, I desiderate, as ground of hope, such a conviction of sin as shuts one out from all hope apart from the grace of God in Christ; such anxiety as is mainly concerned with the question, "How can God be glorified in my salvation?" such consciousness of revived sin, as makes one feel his need of being born again of God, in order to the knowledge and reception of Christ, as He is revealed and offered in the gospel; such acquaintance with Christ, as solves his difficulty as to how his salvation can be to the praise of God's glory, as well as be suitable to his whole case as a sinner, guilty, polluted, and helpless; such a state of feeling towards Christ, that his great desire is to "win Him, and be found in Him;" such faith in Christ, as has the testimony of God regarding Him, as its only warrant; and such effect of believing, that he seeks to be undivided in heart in consecrating himself to the service of God, as one under law to Christ. These, in my judgment, are the essentials of conversion experience;

and I am persuaded that my standard is scriptural. These are the things I would desire to find, in order to have, at the outset, a hope of one having been "turned from darkness unto light, and from the power of Satan unto God." I do not expect to find these things as parts of a detailed process in every case of conversion. I know that the Spirit of God can compress these things into a moment of His working. If I have the result, I need not be careful to know, step by step, how that has been reached. If the fruit that evidences a saving change is produced, I have better ground for a favourable judgment than I could have in a persuasion that all these things were in the process which led to it. But before the result avails for evidence, I cannot, while such experience as I have described is not before me, have hope of a good and abiding result. It is by such a standard as this I have tried the cases of conversion which Dr. Bonar and others have described, in their accounts of the recent movement. If I were to be guided by the descriptions, in my estimate of the cases, I could not, with that standard in my eye, regard them hopefully. I can say with confidence that, in none of the descriptions given, have I seen an account of a change, of which I was not conscious, ere I ever " knew the grace of God in truth." At the same time, I have tried to hope that the cases were sometimes better than the descriptions represented them to be.

DR. BONAR ON THE QUESTION OF DOCTRINE

I WILL not again go along the line of my former remarks as to the doctrine which was the means of promoting the recent excitement. My charges against it have been met only by unreasoned contradictions, and by declarations of the soundness of men, whose orthodoxy I never questioned. To these I cannot attach much importance, especially as Dr. Bonar, in conducting his defence, seems to have adopted the very views which I condemned. This is too amply proved by specimens of his views and teaching, given by him in his pamphlet, and in *The Times of Blessing*. I wish I could have avoided all reference to these; but he has compelled me to notice them. He has doubly done so. He meets, with flat denials, all that I advanced against the teaching to which I referred. I must, therefore, vindicate my statements, though in doing so, I must endeavour to show that what I condemned, as the teaching of another, is held by Dr. Bonar himself. And he charges me with Hyper-Calvinism. I must, therefore, inquire what his own views are; for the measure, in which he declares my views to be extreme, is that in which they differ from his own, as those of a professedly sound Calvinist. I must, therefore, inquire what he holds, that I may show that I need not be a Hyper-Calvinist in order to be greatly above the position which he chooses to occupy. The measure, in which I succeed, will serve to show the dangerous influence of the teaching, against which I issued a warning.

HYPER-EVANGELISM IN DR. BONAR'S PAMPHLET

1. An epitome of his views.

In one paragraph of his pamphlet, he gives an epitome of his views. He does so in order to show that they differ from those which I condemned. He might not have taken the trouble of writing his creed, and it would have been wise to refrain from the attempt; for no one placed him on his defence, and what he has given is, after all, very far from being satisfactory. For his statement of doctrine raises questions not a few.—*The Old Gospel*, p. 56.

What is the difference between the *blood* and the *righteousness* of Christ? and how does "efficacy" attach to the one rather than to the other?

What is meant by a "*world-wide*" gospel as distinguished from a "*free*" gospel? Is it in fact "world-wide" as surely as it is "free?" Or if it is "world-wide" only as "free" to all classes of men who hear it, what are the differing ideas in these two words? It is of consequence to remember that it is not yet world-wide. Its dispensation is as sovereign as its salvation. It is He who "will have mercy on whom He will," who determines by whom it shall be heard, as surely as by whom it shall be believed. The partial distribution of gospel-preaching is a standing witness to the sovereignty of gospel grace.

How is peace with God the *immediate* result of a believed gospel? Is it so as one of the privileges of the believer's state as "in Christ," or is it so as something affecting the believer's consciousness? If the former, does it "flow directly from the light of the cross?" If the latter, how does it come to the believer's heart? Does Dr. Bonar teach that, either as a privilege or as a feeling, peace is obtained without the grace of God being in the heart? Does an assurance of being in a state of peace with God, come to one directly through the faith of the gospel? There is, at any rate, a haze here where haze there should not be. Will Dr. Bonar allow me to interpret his words as meaning that "the light from the cross" shows the way of peace; that in that light the eye of faith discovers that way; that peace with God, as a privilege of their state, is assured by promise to all who believe; and that, according to the measure of their faith in Christ crucified, there is a hope of peace with God, and joy resulting from that hope.

2. The connection of faith and repentance.

I cannot pass over what Dr. Bonar writes as to the connection of faith and repentance. He seems to shrink from plainly saying that the only repentance to be desiderated is that which flows from faith. All he ventures to say is, that any other repentance "must be simply that of the natural conscience" (*The Old Gospel,* p. 62), and he leaves the impression that he regards it, therefore, as something which may be ignored. I would like to know what his view is of the repentance Christ required of those to whom He preached the gospel in Galilee, and Peter, when he preached in His name on the day of Pentecost. Does he hold that there is no change of view, and feeling, and exercise to be desired before faith; and that there is no such change implied in faith, as well as resulting from it? One version of Christ's call is "Repent" (Matt. 4:17); another is "Repent ye and believe the Gospel" (Mark 1:15). Surely, then, there is a repentance preliminary to faith, when Christ says, "Repent and believe;" and there must be repentance involved in faith, when the word "repent" covers the meaning of the word "believe," in that version of the call in which it stands alone. "Repentance unto life," as described in our Shorter Catechism, cannot be without prevenient faith. Only the life, exercised in faith, can be duly affected towards God and towards sin; and it is only the exercise of that life in faith that can bring the fitting influence to bear upon it, in order to produce the exercise of repentance as "a saving grace." But has Dr. Bonar really come to think that it is necessary to confine repentance entirely to this, in order to conserve the free grace of the gospel? It would seem that this is his opinion, for he insists that there was no conviction of sin through the law in the case of the Pentecost converts. "In the Acts of the Apostles," he writes, "we have many specimens of apostolical preaching to promiscuous multitudes, yet, in not one of them is the law introduced. The apostles confined themselves to the glad tidings concerning Christ and His cross. Christ crucified was that which was preached for conviction and conversion. Peter did not say to his hearers, 'Ye have broken the ten commandments, but ye have crucified Christ.' This was the sword which the apostles used for smiting the sinner's conscience; this was the hammer which they brought down with such awful force upon his head."—*The Old Gospel*, p. 59. There was, then, no conviction of sin in cases of conversion under the apostles' preaching! If no law was preached there could not be, "for by the law is the knowledge of sin." But if there was no conviction, there could be no conversion, for conviction of sin is the first step of the work as Christ describes it (John 16:8). Does Dr. Bonar really hold, that the law of God was not applied to the conscience of those who were convinced of their sin in crucifying "the Lord of glory?" "I do not ignore the law," he says, and yet he holds that there can be conviction of sin without it; or, if not, he holds that there can be conversion without conviction, and this is opposed to the teaching of Christ, that one can be "effectually called" without being convinced "of sin and misery," and this is opposed to the doctrine of "the Shorter Catechism."

And a mode of preaching, in which the law is ignored, he regards as necessary, in order to being "as evangelical as Paul," preaching as free a gospel, and saying as broadly and unconditionally as he did at Antioch, in a sermon where *no mention of law* or of sovereignty is made, "By Him all that believe are justified from all things" (p. 59). *"No mention of sovereignty!"* And yet the sermon thus begins, "The God of this people of Israel chose our fathers, and exalted the people when they dwelt as strangers in the land of Egypt, and with an high arm brought He them out of it. And about the time of forty years suffered He their manners in the wilderness. And when He had destroyed

126

seven nations in the land of Canaan, He divided their land to them by lot" (Acts 13:17-19). *"No mention of law!"* And yet the words, immediately following those which he quotes, are "from which ye could not be justified by the law of Moses;" the whole passage being followed by the awful warning with which the sermon was closed: "Beware, therefore, lest that come upon you, which is spoken of in the prophets; Behold, ye despisers, and wonder and perish: for I work a work in your days, a work which ye shall in no wise believe, though a man declare it unto you."

Dr. Bonar has been more affected than I before imagined he ever could be, by his association with those who think that the *anomian* form of preaching is the only one in which the freeness of the gospel can be preserved. He should be far above the weakness of imagining that there can be any appreciation of gospel grace without conviction of sin, and would, if he were himself, and not what he has been shaped into by the pressure of his associates. Of what avail is all the revelation of law which we have in the Book of God? Has not the Spirit prepared it as an instrument to be used in His work? May we not know what the work is, from the form of the instrument with which it is done? Is not Christ's description of the Spirit's work the true one? Does He not tell us that the Comforter convinces "of sin," as well as "of righteousness and judgement?" Can there possibly be an intelligent exercise of faith without this, be it the attainment of a moment, or the result of a process extending through years? And does Dr. Bonar think that he fences the freeness of the gospel by decrying "law-work?" I had always thought that the Spirit of God was a better judge of the mode in which the grace of the gospel should be exhibited and conserved, than a council of all men could be. He has given the clear and awful revelation of the law, in order to "shut" sinners "up to the faith of the gospel." He hath brought it in, "that the offence might abound;" and it is "where sin abounded, grace did much more abound." It is only when this design takes effect on a soul that the grace of God can possibly be known. "Without the law," Paul says, "I was alive," and "sin was dead." It was "when the commandment came, sin revived, and" he "died;" and only after being thus "dead to the law" did he become "alive unto God." Paul's favourite converts in Thessalonica "received the word *in much affliction*, with joy of the Holy Ghost."

I can easily discover why, in some cases, there is such a tendency to an evasion of "law-work." Its effect is so to convince one of sin as to shut him up to blood and to mercy for pardon, to make felt the awful power of sin in the heart, and thus to shut him up to the necessity of being born of God. To be shut up to blood which can meet the demands of divine justice, is to be shut up to the necessity, in order to hope, of discerning Jesus of Nazareth to be the Christ, and the Son of God. To be shut up to mercy is to be in the presence of a Sovereign God. To be sensible of the power of spiritual death is to feel oneself entirely at the disposal of Him who "will have mercy on whom He will," and who alone can, by His Spirit, cause a dead soul to live. Such a case would become utterly unmanageable by human hands. The most urgent pressing to belief in gospel propositions would not help such a soul. Plying such a one with all the skill an evangelised rationalism could bring to bear upon him, would be weak against his difficulties. Such a case must, therefore, if possible, be prevented. Law-work must be decried. There must be a shorter and an easier method of converting men. There must be only such a state of feeling as can be quieted by such belief in gospel statements as an unrenewed man can yield. The anxious are taught that faith is mere belief, and no more. So even Dr. Bonar took pains to teach them; and he has given us a specimen of this as the kind of teaching that was helpful in the "Inquiry room" in bringing souls to peace. Verily, their anxiety must have been a very superficial thing, if this sufficed to give them peace. And when such peace as this kind of faith secures is enjoyed, they who attain to it are told that they are converts. Some wonder, and some give thanks that this result was so easily and so soon attained. And they think this was because of the care taken to exhibit the freeness of the gospel. The facility was rather due to a substitute for gospel grace. Faith, and not Christ, was the Saviour preached to them. Believing was said to be an easy thing to do, and so they found it; and they did their believing in as self-righteous a spirit as if they had been doing Popish penance.

3. Sudden conversions.

"*All conversions must be sudden, if they are the work of the Holy Ghost.*" This sentence Dr. Bonar has given in italics, that he might emphasise it, and draw to it the reader's eye. To this doctrine, at any rate, he commits himself. And what does he mean by conversion? He calls it *the work* of the Holy Ghost, and must allow that it is done by Him, in order to the turning of a sinner "*from* darkness *unto* light, and *from* the power of Satan *unto* God." This whole work "must be sudden," he says, "if it is the work of the Holy Ghost." No one, therefore, according to Dr. Bonar, has been truly converted unto God, who has not been suddenly converted. The Spirit invariably does His work suddenly. Then Luther and Bunyan were never converted, for the process through which they passed was a very protracted one; and there can be no hope reserved for them, because this rule admits of no exceptions. So says Dr. Bonar. But he cannot surely mean what he says. He perhaps intended to say that the act of faith in which conversion work results is a sudden thing, or that the regenerating act of the Holy Ghost which immediately produced that faith was done in a moment. If this is what he meant, it would surely have been better to say so, than to extend his extravagant statement as a shield over dangerous error.

I said before, and I repeat, that there have been sudden conversions since the days of the apostles, as there had been then; and the seeming instances of this recorded in "The days of the Fathers in Ross-shire," and which Dr. Bonar has quoted, I gave, just because they were exceptional. The Word of God has not laid down the rule of sudden conversion, and the antecedents of the work of God have not established it since.

HYPER-EVANGELISM IN THE INQUIRY-ROOM

Dr. Bonar has supplied me with the information which he alleges I lacked, by not attending the inquiry-rooms. He has given, from his own hand, samples of the teaching which is dealt out to those who frequent them. He cannot challenge the evidence thus provided; and he must allow that I may fairly judge of how souls are treated there, if what he himself has given is taken as a specimen. I refer to articles from Dr. Bonar's pen in *The Times of Blessing*.

Judging from the information thus furnished, it appears—

1. That great pains are taken to instruct inquirers regarding faith.
2. That the faith recommended to them is mere belief.
3. That they are assured that this belief infallibly secures their salvation.
4. That the consciousness of this belief is of itself a sufficient basis for an assurance of being in a state of peace with God.

1. *Great pains are taken to inform inquirers as to the nature of faith.* This is so far well. But there is a danger of substituting faith, in this painstaking, for Christ. If I might judge from Dr. Bonar's account, there is reason to apprehend that this danger has never been seen, far less feared and avoided, by those who lead in "the Inquiry-room." Faith is represented as something to be done, in order to salvation; and pains are taken to show that it is an easy thing. Better far than this would it be to see to it, that those with whom they deal are truly convinced of sin, and to labour to set forth Christ before them, in His glorious completeness as a Saviour. To explain faith to them, that they may do it, is to set them still to work, though setting an easier task before them. I know well the tendency there is, at a certain stage of anxious inquiry, to ask, "What is faith, that I may do it?" It is a legalist's work to satisfy that craving; but this is what is done in the "Inquiry-room." "Who is he, that I may believe in him?" was the question asked by one who approached the dawning of a day of salvation. Explanations of what faith is are but trifling with souls. How different is the Scripture way! The great aim there is to "set forth" the object, not to explain the act, of faith. Let there be conviction, illumination, and renewal, and faith becomes the instinctive response of the quickened soul to the presentation by God of His Christ; and, without these, no explanations of faith can be helpful to any one. The labour to explain it is too often adapted to the craving of a legal spirit. It were wiser to take pains in removing ignorance and error regarding God, and sin, and Christ. Help them to know these, if you would not build them up with "untempered mortar" in a false peace. If you would be wise, as well as kind, work in that direction, rather than in the hurrying of them to belief.

It may be said, "Surely instruction is needful as to what faith is, and it should therefore be given." Yes, and so far Scripture is your guide in explaining it. But how does Scripture direct you to explain it? As something opposed to working, not as something which is itself an easy work. Scripture represents it as something which is not working at all, but receiving—as a ceasing from works to become a debtor for all to grace. "To him that worketh not, but believeth in Him that justifieth the ungodly, his faith is counted for righteousness." But it is impossible for those, who view it as Dr. Bonar represents it, thus to explain it; for,

2. The faith which he recommends in the Inquiry-room is mere belief. This he again and again repeats. An inquirer asks, "Am I then to take faith and believing just in their usual meaning, as when they are applied to the things of man?" To this question the answer is, "Of course." "Is my believing what a friend writes to me, the same as my believing what God writes to me?" the inquirer asks, and the answer is, "It is." At last the inquirer is brought to say, "I see it. In believing,

I AM JUSTIFIED; and God uses the word believing with the common meaning which I, as a man, attach to it every day in common things."— *Times of Blessing,* p. 82. In his whole dealing with this inquirer, Dr. Bonar laboured to confine him to the idea of belief as the only one implied in faith. But how can the word *"believe"* mean this, and no more, in the words, "Believe in the Lord Jesus Christ, and thou shalt be saved." Is not faith represented in Scripture as trust, as well as belief? Is not faith a receiving of Jesus Christ, as well as a believing in His name (John 1:12)? If it be belief, and no more, its value must entirely depend on its character, as an act or exercise of soul. Separate belief from the ideas of reception and trust, and press one to the exercise of it, and you but direct him to seek a ground of hope in his own act. Mere belief leaves me still within myself. It is as my act alone it secures my salvation. In mere belief, I pass not out of myself to Christ. This cannot be the faith of the gospel, which is "to the saving of the soul." That faith reaches salvation only by coming to Christ. It receives Him and rests on Him. Only as I do so in the exercise of faith do I cease from working. Only as I do so can my wearied soul find rest.

Dr. Bonar is careful to distinguish between *"realising"* and *"believing"* the gospel. He represents the desire to realise the gospel on the part of an inquirer as a hindrance to believing. Surely there is danger in such teaching as this. Realising a thing is having it as a reality before one's mind. This, surely, is not a thing to be separated from faith, far less to be regarded as a hindrance to it. If he meant that it was not right to desire to have the heart impressed by the objects of faith, before they were realised by faith, he ought expressly to have said so. If what he meant to teach was that the benefits, proffered in the gospel, cannot be enjoyed, till they are realised and appropriated by faith he ought to have distinctly said so. To appear to say, that the objects of faith are not as realities before the believer's mind, is just to appear to say, that they are not believed at all. For "faith is the substance of things hoped for, the evidence of things not seen." And are you to repress the desire for an experience through faith of the effectual working of the word in the heart? That which does not realise "the things of God" may be belief, but it is not true faith; and the faith is dead that does not result in the effectual working of the gospel in the heart.

It is of no avail to tell us that the other aspects of faith were held, though in reserve. Should they have been in reserve while dealing with inquirers? And if faith is declared to be belief and no more, how can they be held at all?

Nor will it avail to refer to what is said, in another paper, regarding Jesus Christ, the Son of God, being the object of faith, if it be mere belief regarding Him that is recommended. If there be no reception of, and no trust in, Him, what makes this faith to differ from that of the unclean spirit, who exclaimed, "I know Thee, who Thou art, the Holy One of God."

3. In the Inquiry-room souls are assured that salvation is infallibly secured by this faith, which they may have in common with the despairing spirits of darkness. This is surely not safe teaching. Salvation secured without the reception of Christ! Salvation reached in a way that makes no provision for a personal interest in His finished work! Salvation without union to the Head in whom all fullness dwelleth! And this must be implied in the teaching that ignores faith as a coming to Christ, and as "a receiving and resting on Him alone for salvation, as He is freely offered to us in the gospel." Salvation secured by a work, called belief, which an unrenewed man finds to be easy, and which is done in the same state of feeling, in which he receives as true the letter of a friend conveying to him the gossip of the day! This may be "the old gospel" of the Inquiry-room, but it is not the ever new and everlasting gospel of the grace of GOD. It is "old" enough, but instead of being "gospel," it is legalism with scarce a rag to cover it.

4. The consciousness of this faith is declared to be a sufficient basis for an assurance of being in a state of peace with God. "On God's authority, I am assured that 'he who believeth is justified.' I believe, and so I must come to the sure conclusion that I am justified." Thus taught Dr. Bonar in the Inquiry-room. There is surely some great confusion here. Assurance of my being called to Christ, in order to have peace with God through His blood, is directly conveyed by the gospel. A warrant for that assurance there is, quite irrespective even of my faith. But to say that an assurance, of being in a state of peace, is irrespective of the grace of God in the heart, is surely dangerous doctrine. True, if I am justified by faith I have peace with God. True, if justified, it is by faith and not by works, nor by feelings, nor by regeneration, "but only for the righteousness of Christ imputed to us, and received by faith alone." But how am I to ascertain that I have believed; for, if I have not ascertained this, I cannot be assured that I am justified. Is it enough to say, "I am conscious of faith, and therefore I am assured of justification?" The consciousness of faith does certainly occasion a hope of justification; but even this is a consciousness of grace in the heart. But if the question should arise, "Is my faith genuine?" how am I to deal with it? Am I to put it down as a temptation to doubt? Or am I to examine whether my faith proves itself genuine by its fruits? Verily this latter is the course to which the word of God directs me in multiplied passages. "Faith without works is dead;" and my conscience cannot lawfully accept it "without works" as sufficient, to whatever extent I am conscious of it, as evidence of my being in a state of peace with God. True, the consciousness of a new state of feeling, as the effect of faith, may be good evidence of its genuineness, before there can be a course of action to attest it. But it is the accrediting of faith by works, which alone can form a basis for a steadfast assurance of having "passed from death to life" (2 Pet. 1:1-10). "We know that we have passed from death to life, because we love the brethren," and the love which is evidence of this change, is not "in word, neither in tongue; but in deed and in truth" (1 John 3:14, 18).

The views which I have referred to, though found in Dr. Bonar's writings, are not his standing opinions. They are only his temporary aberrations from the line of orthodoxy. They indicate the shape which his teaching has assumed under pressure from without. But a step by him marks a league by another.

DR BONAR'S DEFENCE OF THE NEW DEVICES

1. Silent Prayer

The silent prayer, he first defends. He charges me with saying that there should be no prayer but in the closet and in the public congregation. I never thought or said so. But I did say, and I repeat, that to "assume an attitude of prayer," in open assembly, to pray individually and silently, is contrary to the mind of Christ; for it is doing before men what Christ directed to be done only in the closet. Those who are careful to preserve a praying frame of spirit, and who are in the habit of sending heart-bolts of prayer heavenwards, do not feel dependent on this formality and are the least likely to be given to it. A consciousness of a blank, the result of neglect, there must be where there is an attempt to fill it by "voluntary" service such as this, except in the case of those who do it just because it has become the church fashion. Where there is a healthy sense of shortcoming, it is not in this way one would care to eke the deficit.

Dr. Bonar's attempt to find support for "the silent prayer" practice, in "the Directory for Public Worship," is a failure. It forbids those who come in late to engage in private devotions, therefore, he says, "it takes for granted that those who come in early may do so." The plainer inference is, that it was becoming a habit for those who came in, after the public preliminary services were over, to endeavour to make up for what they lost through their laziness, by engaging in silent prayer. This it condemns; and to this extent alone, as to this matter, does it give any direction whatever. If to do it at the outset was deemed proper, why was a direction to do it omitted?

2. The Inquiry Meeting

As to the *Inquiry Meeting*, Dr. Bonar declares that it is no new thing, and this is really all that he adduces to justify it. Of attempts, amidst excitement, and in haste to classify into inquirers and converts those who were impressed, he shrinks from undertaking the defence. He passes, from what is done in the Inquiry-room, to what is afterwards done in the session-house, and in "the study," in dealing with applicants for admission to the table of the Lord. The work of examining them, in the latter case, may, as Dr. Bonar alleges, have been carefully done. But those who then examined with such care, most emphatically condemned what was done in the Inquiry-room. To be careful at that stage cannot justify being lax at an earlier; yea, the later care is a condemnation of the earlier neglect. To admit applicants to sealing ordinances is something very different from telling them that they are converts. They, who do admit them, have no right to make any such declaration, even when satisfied as to their right, before the church, to the privilege which they ask. But, without examination, at the earlier stage this declaration was publicly made. They who professed to have found peace were proclaimed in their own hearing, and, in some instances, in the hearing of thousands, to be converts. "The Inquiry-room," it may be said, is, according to its name, merely a place for inquirers and not for converts. True, but they have been separated both from the converts and from the careless ere they entered it. And how often, after having been pressed to an avowal of faith, have they been told that they were converts, and have thanks been rendered in their presence, to God for their conversion. Tickets of different colours have sometimes been given to inquirers and converts to mark the distinction between them; and the latter have been induced to stand up before thousands to make a public declaration of their faith. It may have been regarded as a wise thing, by a little dexterity, thus to commit them; but was it wise, thus to commit the cause of Christ, before the world, to cases such as these. And all this has been done without even the pretence of any ecclesiastical action bearing upon the impressed in the way of examination and training. These things may be an outcome of fervent zeal, but they are evidences of presumption and folly.

The Inquiry-room service, if an extension of the work of the public assembly, is unnecessary. If a substitute for private dealing with individuals, it is too public. In any case, it cannot admit of due care being taken in dealing with souls individually, as to their eternal interests. There must be haste and perfunctoriness in the performance of the work done, and very often undue pressure and excitement. There must be a "healing slightly" of wounds, a coarse hurried daubing with untempered mortar. The structures reared by builders there are not likely to be enduring. How little depth and solemnity of feeling can there be in the heart of one, who, in the presence of others, can expose his case to a hasty handling, by whatever person comes to speak to him, about his soul's salvation! The crowding of an Inquiry-room is, of itself, sufficient proof of the superficiality of the impression, made in the open assembly. Far better, than a rush to the Inquiry-room, would be a quiet retiring to the closet to be there alone with God and His Word. If there were less dependence on an arm of flesh, there would be fewer in the Inquiry-room; and if men had more reliance on the Spirit of God, and less on themselves, there would be less desire to have it filled.

3. THE OPEN MEETING

As to the *Open Meeting,* Dr. Bonar deemed it unnecessary to do more in its defence, than to quote a description given by me of a meeting in the North, which is *not* open. He must have been blindly anxious for a retort when he could make use of this. An open meeting is a thing utterly unknown in the Highlands. A strange affair it would become if it were started! It is true that at our "fellowship meetings," there is a question called for, without any one being asked by name to propose it. But this liberty is carefully limited, generally to the public speakers, and always to male communicants. To the question, thus proposed, no one speaks except one called to do so by the presiding minister. Is this an open meeting? I know enough of the anxiety of unqualified men, and women too, to speak, and I have seen enough of the open meeting practice, both in this country and in America, to assure me of the wisdom of our fathers, in taking care that no such institution should be started.

4. THE ORGAN

Dr. Bonar does not defend *the organ,* neither will he condemn it. "It was a mere appendage," he says, "and a very small one." He inverts the telescope when he looks at anything connected with the movement, which he cannot approve. Yes, Dr. Bonar has already come to think of it as "a small" thing; but many of his friends have attained to thinking it a *good* thing. He is not quite so far behind, however, but he can follow them. "We have not introduced it into our Church services." Not yet; but you have helped to create a craving to which you will, erewhile, yield that concession.

5. THE HYMNS

As to *the hymns,* Dr. Bonar is still less disposed to defend them. "Many of them are feeble, and some worse than feeble," is his verdict as to the hymns. But they are not "as bad as our paraphrases," he adds, by way of saying something in their favour. Alas! for the paraphrases, if that be true. He asks me to "attack these relics of moderatism, in the Church Courts." It so happens, and Dr. Bonar knows this well, that he sets me to a very hopeless task. Both he and I would be more likely to get rid of them, if we praised them, there. But I have never used a paraphrase in the service of praise. If I cannot displace them I can manage to keep out of their way. I have done so hitherto, and I am likely to do so to the end. I am, therefore, quite free to "assail feeble hymns" wherever I may meet them.

DR. BONAR CHARGES ME WITH HYPER-CALVINISM

INOTICE this, not for the purpose of complaining of an unfounded charge, nor with the view of taking any pains to exculpate myself, but in order to express myself distinctly in reference to the state of mind in which such a suspicion as this originates. The idea that *"law and sovereignty"* must be ignored, in order to the preaching of a "free gospel," as Dr. Bonar seems to think, is one of those weaklings that can only issue from an infant school of theology. Because I will not ignore the sovereignty of God, and the necessity of conviction of sin through the law, in order to shut sinners up to the faith of the gospel, and of spiritual illumination and renewal in order to the reception of Christ, it is imagined that the gospel which I preach cannot be free. These are the things on which I have insisted, and on the ground of which I am called a Hyper-Calvinist. I stay not, though the task is easy, to show that I could not adhere to the Westminster Confession if these were not my views. But I ask Dr. Bonar, does he really think that these things must be dropped out of preaching, in order to its "not repelling those to whom the Saviour says, 'Come unto Me?' " In John 6 we have the model gospel sermon. Are these themes ignored in it? Take that as the test of teaching, and does it warrant your withholding that which is repellent to unrenewed men, in order to win them to faith? What idea of the gospel have the men who think that it is unfit for being *all* preached? What due respect for Christ can they have who do not choose, in their preaching, to follow Him? What faith in the Holy Ghost can they have, who think Him incapable of using effectively, in subduing sinners to Christ, the weapon which He hath prepared for that work? What right idea of the life, which the Spirit hath begotten, can be in the mind that fears it will not take kindly to all that the Spirit hath inspired? The gospel does not need to be pared down, in order to its being effective for gracious ends. And will you ever succeed in fairly exhibiting the grace of God without reference to His sovereignty? Will you ever be helpful in bringing sinners to be debtors to His grace, while refusing to direct them to take their place at His footstool? Will you undertake to bring men to know the grace of God, without their knowing how sinful they are themselves? While hiding from them the law's claims, do you think you can acquaint them with the salvation of the gospel? And what but utter incapacity could fail to see, that to insist on what is required in order to a cordial reception of Christ, as was done in Christ's dealing with Nicodemus, quite harmonises with a clear trumpet ring in proclaiming the call of the gospel to all.

When will some men cease to hamper themselves with the idea, that the call is theirs, and not God's, and that they must reconcile it with their own notions about the relative fitness of things before they issue it? The call is God's, and His ambassadors have but to convey it from His mouth to sinners. And when will other men cease to think, that somehow there must be spiritual ability, to some extent, on the part of those who hear ere their unbelief could be regarded as guilty, and ere the gospel could be preached to them with any reasonable hope of success? Yet these are the men who would assert the dignity of human nature, and who would represent those who will not ignore the spiritual death of sinners, as degrading their fellow-creatures by their estimate of their condition! But how thoroughly reversed is the true state of the case. Those who regard man's rational life as something to which responsibility cannot attach, unless there be added to its capacity the power of another life, are the men who really degrade human nature. He who addresses the reason of men, in the name of God, while realising their utter spiritual impotence, who believes that there is unreasonable wickedness in the unbelief that rejects the salvation of the gospel, on account of which they who are guilty of it may for ever justly perish, is the man who gives to his fellow-men their due place, while reserving His for God. But those others, unduly depreciating the condition of men as rational, and thinking that, in order to constitute them at all responsible, some spiritual power must be superadded to their capacity as reasonable beings, degrade men, and would displace God.

No one, who ignores the sinner's need of regeneration in order to faith, can fully preach "the gospel of the grace of God." It is as I keep in view, both the work required in order to make the word effectual, and the warrant for preaching it to all, that the grace of the Tri-une Jehovah can either shine into my heart, or shine forth in my preaching. I must be zealous for the glory of the Holy Ghost, and specially for the honour of His grace, as surely as for that of the Father and of the Son. For He is one in essence and in love with the Father and the Son. He, in the economy of redemption, has His place and work—a place which only a Divine person can fill, a work which only Divine grace would undertake, and only Divine power could effect. Can I preach the gospel of the grace of God, and ignore that place and work? Can I do so, and preach the "unsearchable riches of Christ?" Is He not Christ, because He hath been anointed with the fullness of the Holy Ghost? Can I preach Him fully, and ignore the work which He hath to accomplish, as an exalted Saviour, by His Spirit on the earth? And can I fitly and fully commend the Father's love, and ignore the greatness of the work which the Spirit, whom He sends in the name of Jesus, has, according to His will, to accomplish? "No man cometh unto" Christ, "except the Father, who hath sent" Him, "draw him." Must I not be careful to show how great that work of the Father's is, which, by the Spirit, He effects, in order to show forth His love to sinners. If, because I am determined thus to preach the grace of the Triune Jehovah, I am to be called a Hyper-Calvinist, let me never cease to be branded with the name. I care not, except in confession to God, to tell how I actually preach the gospel, but it is thus that I fain would always preach it.

Index